ORDEAL OF THE ANIMALS

ORDEAL OF THE ANIMALS

Mel Morse

Prentice-Hall, Inc.
Englewood Cliffs, N.J.

ORDEAL OF THE ANIMALS by Mel Morse Library of Congress Catalog Card Number: 68-16322 Printed in the United States of America • T Prentice-Hall International, Inc., London Prentice-Hall of Australia, Pty. Ltd., Sydney Prentice-Hall of Canada, Ltd., Toronto Prentice-Hall of India Private Ltd., New Delhi Prentice-Hall of Japan, Inc., Tokyo

Foreword

WE DON'T NEED TO BE TOLD OF THE MANY BENEFITS WE derive from the animal kingdom. Our well-being, and often our lives, depend upon a great number and variety of animals. Their unnecessary ordeals in our behalf is an account they have neither the choice nor voice to reveal. Nor it seems, has anyone possessing these powers. Therefore, the public, the real source of reform, has been blinded to the extent and manner of brutality thousands of animals undergo each day in this country. Over many years I have witnessed and worked to prevent the abuse of America's animal life. It is the purpose of this book to expose the ordeal, needless ordeal, of animals, and to show that the use of animals—in science, as food, clothing, as entertainment—can be humane.

I would like to acknowledge gratefully the encouragement of Dr. Joseph Wood Krutch and the Publisher, and the assistance of Kurt Unkelbach in the preparation of this book.

My activity in the field of animal welfare has been furthered by the understanding of my wife and family and the support of many humanitarians. To them I dedicate this book.

MEL MORSE

Introduction

Most people are aware that in the United States there are laws against cruelty to animals, as well as various organizations devoted to animal welfare. They may occasionally read in their newspapers that someone has been fined for some outrageous barbarity, but such a bit of news only confirms their comfortable assumption that the laws are adequate and functioning.

Anyone with such an opinion is due for a shock when he reads this book. Every day, almost every hour, helpless animals are undergoing terrible ordeals. They are neglected, tormented for sport, or subjected to ingenious tortures in laboratories. The laws are inadequate, and inadequately enforced, and they remain so partly because men and women of good will are ignorant or inactive while those who profit from the various cruelties actively oppose new regulations or nullify their effectiveness by supporting amendments or the refusal to vote adequate funds for enforcement. With the publication of this book no one need remain ignorant or complacent.

Cockfights, dogfights, and the rest may be only faint survivals from a brutal past when thousands of animals were slaughtered at a single performance in the Roman arena or every available kind of animal suffered in Elizabethan bear rings to titillate the sadistic lusts of the public. What was open and frequent and respectable then, is now usually more or less clandestine, though still more common than most people imagine. But, as is often the case in our society, new evils have arisen to take the place of those which have been controlled. We have no Coliseum and no advertised bear rings. Even bullfighting, though regarded in some circles as a smart spectator sport, is illegal in the United States. But private torture behind closed doors has probably never before flourished so widely as it now does in scores of laboratories, including those in grammar and high schools.

Of all the forms of deliberate cruelty prevalent those which take place under the banner of Science are the most nearly immune to criticism. Once the Inquisition was not only tolerated but justified because it was supposed to operate in defense of a Church beyond criticism. Today Science is similarly sacrosanct. Whatever is done in a laboratory by men who call themselves scientists is assumed to be justified. Scientists are assumed to be intelligent and dedicated men. They would not torture an animal unless there were compelling reasons for doing so. Do we not owe to their investigations the blessings of modern medicine?

Such comfortable convictions can hardly survive the evidence of this book. And yet, though the United States is far behind England, where many leading scientists have criticized our apparent inhumanity in the name of Science, attempts to bring our laws up to minimum standards are being actively resisted by special interests.

Animal abuse is widespread and various in the United States. It goes under many names, "Science" being only one. Entertainment, commerce, even religion, are some

Contents

Preface

If a future historian bases his judgment of us on printed matter—today's scientific journals and humane society reports—he could hardly be blamed for classifying us as well-dressed barbarians. We pollute our air, we poison our waters, we waste our natural resources, and torture all lesser animals.

What's to blame? Our heritage?

Sometimes it seems that way. From the time of the first white settlers, ours has been considered the land of plenty. Nature's abundance was everywhere, and succeeding generations made destruction a popular pastime. It took a few hundred years, but the great herds and flocks are gone now: sturgeon no longer flourish in our rivers, and too many forms of life have been hunted into extinction. Indifference has been our heritage, and now—in this enlightened century—we remain true to that tradition.

John Doe, a fine family man and a good citizen, kisses his wife and children good-bye, plays with Rover, then departs for work. He's fond of Rover, treats the dog like a member of the family. He worries when the pet's eyes are watery. Their close relationship—a man and his beloved dog—does not influence John's daily work at the laboratory. Today he will probably scald or beat a few dogs to determine the precise amount of punishment they can take before losing consciousness. He did the same thing last

Friday and he'll do it again tomorrow, or until he's used up all the canines purchased for this particular research. Others have conducted this research tens of thousands of times, and John has enough data to fill a library, but he wants to be sure. He's also an organized man, and wants to complete the experiment before moving on to his next project, a simple matter of bleeding a hundred dogs and cats to death. The animal blood will be needed for the testing of some heart machines.

John Blank, one of the best horsemen in all the West, exhibits extreme devotion for his favorite mount. The man loves his horse and does everything possible to protect him as they go about their business of pursuing, crippling and then driving wild horses to the slaughterhouse. Of course, there aren't many wild horses left, so there aren't many John Blanks, and one seldom reads about them.

But everybody knows about the John Goldbrick type, for his name makes news all through the year and especially at Kentucky Derby time. The wealthy holder of one of America's most illustrious family names, this John—important enough in his own right to dine at the White House several times a year—will consider his life unfulfilled if a horse carrying his colors does not win the Derby. He's been around horses and tracks all his life. Can it be that he doesn't know the risks involved in racing two-year-olds? That it's foolish and ridiculous and dangerous to pressure those young bones? Doesn't he care about horses—even his own?

John Baron can't match Goldbrick in family name,

but he can match him in dollars any day in the week. Baron's spread is the biggest in his state, and he's the first to admit that he'd be a nobody today if it weren't for his cattle. "My livelihood?" he's fond of saying to interviewers. "Hell, cattle are my life. I owe everything to cattle." He's been known to say that while supervising the use of such instruments as the branding iron, the castration knife, and the dehorning shears. And if the interviewer is from an important magazine, Baron will even place his mother on a par with his cattle: "I owe her a lot, too. She raised me to be a moral man, and considerate of others, if you know what I mean." And he's been known to say that while sitting on a rail, drink in hand, cheering on his hired hands as they practice their skills for the rodeo circuit: roping, throwing and tying young cattle or goats, spurring their horses, and tightening the painful flanking straps.

Doe, Blank, Goldbrick and Baron all think that something should be done about the poultry industry. They consider the keeping of hens in battery cages to be cruelty of the first order. Just as cruel as cockfights. They probably wouldn't approve of dogfights, either, but then they may not know about that thriving sport.

Not many people do. Yet this senseless fighting to the death of maddened canines for the amusement of human spectators continues to thrive across America. The sport, to call it by its least appropriate name, is popular enough to support several magazines. Anyone may subscribe to these magazines, and also to the publications devoted to cockfighting. Coming fight dates and places are announced in the pages of both. All have second-class mailing privileges, and the postal department is happy to deliver them, as it has for so many years.

Never let it be said that America, whatever it does to its animals, is not a sporting nation.

Anything Goes 1

At least two million American families will be saddened this year because beloved pets are missing. Each family will search in its own fashion, and they will remain hopeful for varying lengths of time. The searching and the hoping will be useless. The missing cats and dogs will never be seen by their human families again.

The bitter truth is that pet stealing is a big business. The pet-stealer's marketplace is the research laboratory, and the appetite for animals of that house of science is insatiable. The two million stolen cats and dogs will be just that many drops in the bucket. At least 500,000,000 more animals will be required each year for experiments that are designed to benefit man and to enhance his knowledge.

What awaits these animals when they arrive at the laboratories? Consider first our halls of learning:

Harvard University, where a special fireproof room was built so that the fine art of burns might better be understood by man. In this chamber, "lightly" anesthetized pigs were strapped on a steel grill just a few inches above shallow pans of gasoline. The gasoline, ignited by an electric spark, produced temperatures as high as 900 degrees Centigrade. Once burned, the pigs were given no further sedative or anesthetic, and some survived for four more days. Then there were the dogs who were forced to breathe air heated to 500 degrees Centigrade, and the other dogs who were forced to breathe actual flames.

Loma Linda University of Los Angeles, where faculty members used a heart-lung machine for performing open-heart surgery on several dozen dogs. While the surgery was performed under anesthesia of a sort, unnecessary suffering resulted because of crude surgical procedures, and none of the dogs was given postoperative care. Virtually every dog used in this experiment died within two days.

Experiment? Not really. Similar surgery had already been conducted on thousands of dogs in other research laboratories. Indeed, the faculty members admitted under oath that their work was not experimental and could not produce new scientific knowledge.

The University of Michigan conducted an experiment in which cats were repeatedly struck on the head. The blows were delivered by a pneumatic hammer driven by compressed nitrogen. Although the cats were given a relaxant to reduce their motor activity and facilitate their handling, they were not unconscious when they were beaten, and none of them received anesthetic after undergoing the brutality. All of the cats suffered severe brain concussions, as anticipated.

St. Louis University managed to produce brain concussions in dogs by delivering "multiple blows to the head with a 16-ounce hammer and by electrical detonations of a blasting cap taped to the animal's scalp." The dogs were given "light Nembutal anesthesia" during the acute stages of the experiment, but none later. It is uncertain whether neurosurgery benefited from all this.

Creighton University starved groups of dogs for periods of up to 65 days. When the famished animals were at last given food, they "often appeared ill or in pain." Furthermore, some of the dogs suffered convulsions, or diarrhea, or vomiting.

The University of Pennsylvania reported a "standardized back burn procedure," in which rats were immersed in water heated to a few degrees below the boiling point. The scalding of animals is so common a laboratory enterprise that it now has a standard of its own.

Cornell University researchers surgically destroyed the senses of sight, hearing and smell in a small army of cats. Over a period of ten years, the mutilated cats were subjected to electric shocks, blows on the face, pinching of the tail, and other major and minor torments. All this in the interest of neurology: just what was learned in these ten years is not clear.

Johns Hopkins University, involved in research of nervous and mental diseases, concentrated on a single cat: "During the 139 days of survival, the cat was subjected, every two or three days, to a variety of noxious stimuli. On one occasion the tail, shaved and moistened, was stimulated tetanically (causing painful spasms as those of tetanus) through electrodes. At the end of a 5-second stimulation, the cat screamed loudly and spat twice. The last of these stimulations produced a third-degree electrical burn of the tail." The same cat also screamed when a large surgical clamp was applied to its tail. After 139 days of this type of torture, the cat died, leaving us the knowledge that the feline tail has a nervous system.

When one laboratory's research on animals establishes something significant, scores of other laboratories repeat the experiment, and more thousands of animals are needlessly tortured and killed. The list of university laboratories conducting needlessly cruel experiments is not endless, but it is lengthy. The story is much the same in hundreds of other research laboratories not associated with universities around the land. Every day of the year, hundreds and often thousands of fully conscious animals are scalded, or beaten, or crushed to death, and more are subjected to exotic surgery and then allowed to die slowly and in agony.

It's all in the records. The undeniable proof is there. It's in the daily press, too, but one must search for it—Hollywood divorces, new fashions, hippies, LSD, and gambling rate much more space. The best laboratory coverage is found in the scientific publications, and one must read one such as the *American Journal of Physiology* to learn about the New York City experiment conducted by a team of eminent researchers interested in massive irradiation of the head. A known lethal dose of radiation was applied to the heads of 18 dogs and every one of them, after up to 28 hours of acute pain and nausea, died. The same lethal dose had already been tried on mice, guinea pigs, rabbits and monkeys, and the results had been identical. For some reason, rats were overlooked, though there are almost as many rats as people in the big city.

On occasion, some of the daily papers do report in detail, and of these *The New York Times* is the best example. The readers of that newspaper can be sure of keeping reasonably up to date on such experiments as the one conducted by a famous endocrinologist on more than 15,000 rats. He was studying the effects of extreme stress and hoped to demonstrate that all forms of physical and neurological stress produced similar or identical terminal effects. Before he ran out of new ways to torture rats to death, 14 years had passed and 15,000 rats had died. Any scientist could have told the endocrinologist that a few hundred rats, at the most, would have proved his point, and that the point itself was not new. But except for the years involved, this was not an unusual case. At this very moment, some scientist somewhere may be ordering thousands of dogs and cats and monkeys to prove the same point once again. It's curious how curious a scientist can be.

All this and more has been aired in one congressional hearing after the other, but nothing much happens. In fact, sometimes the Government itself is the worst offender. For example:

Long after the University of Pennsylvania had established the standard for scalding animals, the Office of Naval Research supported a scalding experiment with 43 female dogs. The bitches were anesthetized, then dipped into water heated to 185 degrees Fahrenheit. After regaining consciousness, none of the bitches was given anesthesia or sedative. Most died within 24 hours.

The Walter Reed Army Institute of Research, in an apparent effort to prove that pain can be the mother of clear thinking, implanted wire electrodes in the pain areas of the brains of nine monkeys. The monkeys were under anesthesia during the surgery, a kindness that would prove to be ironic. Several days later, the monkeys, all fully conscious, were restrained in steel chairs, and electric current was applied to the implanted electrodes.

"The monkeys showed facial grimacing, closure of both eyes, high-pitched vocalization, and generalized motor activity," reads the report in a euphemistic description of monkeys screaming their pain and struggling madly with their bonds. No one had told the monkeys that there was an escape from all this scientific pain. All they had to do was press a switch and the electric current would automatically diminish. Most of the monkeys found the switch within six hours, and nobody really knows whether they found relief through accident or brilliance. The gruesome experiment was repeated uninterruptedly for 24 hours, and in all that time the monkeys were allowed no food, water, or rest.

But these are only mild examples of Government-sponsored, well-intentioned (perhaps) cruelty. More to the point is the fact that Washington grants over a billion dollars a year to medical research. Much of this research is needed, but far too much of it is needlessly repetitive, and far too much of it—on the laboratory level—is needlessly cruel.

Strangely, or at least it appears strange to the average taxpayer, the billion-plus dollars are granted without supervision or controls. The money is federal, but the laws of most states provide laboratories with immunity from inspection. Thus, old traditions continue, from the simple to the complex. Simple traditions such as the cutting of an animal's vocal cords so that he cannot cry out his pain and alert the immediate neighborhood, or perhaps disturb the researcher. The complex would be any number of instruments specifically designed to make an animal wish he were already dead. The Blalock press and the Noble-Collip drum are fine examples, both of them often used in automobile industry research.

The Blalock is best described as resembling a grape press or an old-fashioned printing press. Through a screw arrangement, two facing metal plates, each boasting rows of dull steel teeth, are forced against each other. The press is used to study the causes and effects of shock. Dogs are commonly used in this experiment, and the general idea is to exert enough pressure to crush the flesh of the legs without breaking the bones. Pressure in the thousands of pounds per square inch can be applied, and in the final stages anesthesia is not given to the dog. He remains in the press for several hours. This method of producing shock is so popular that at one time—if one has faith in medical periodicals—a hundred identical studies were being conducted at as many different laboratories, with a grand total of over 4,000 dogs as unwilling subjects.

That sort of experiment has been going on for a number of years, and when all the information is correlated

Detroit, hopefully, will be able to design a safer automobile. But Ford, General Motors and Washington seem to have their doubts about that, and grants from all three are currently supporting advanced experiments at one university laboratory in the fields of brain concussion and the displacement of body organs as the result of sudden crashes. The experiments take considerable time and effort, so, on an average, only two animals a week are torn apart or battered to death. Thus far, dogs and monkeys are the favorite victims, and—as just one of the tests—time hammers or pneumatic clubs are clamped on their skulls. "The animals must be kept alive during experimentation, because dead tissues react differently than living tissues," reads one report.

Has Congress ever heard about these instruments of torture, and about the Blalock press in particular? The House of Representatives heard about it as far back as 1962 when the late Fred Meyers, executive director of The Humane Society of the United States, reported:

> On the table here, I have an instrument known in medical research circles as the Blalock press. It somewhat resembles, as you can see, an old-fashioned printing press in which one plate can be forced against an opposing face by a screw arrangement. In the Blalock press both plates have rows of dull steel teeth. Transversely, there is a slot about two inches wide.
>
> This press, used in scores of experiments extending over many years, is used to crush the leg of a dog. A hind leg of a dog is inserted in the transverse slot, which is provided so that flesh may be crushed to a pulp without breaking the bones of the leg. The press

can be calibrated so that measurable pressures ranging from 500 to 5,000 pounds per square inch can be exerted.

Let me describe, precisely, the use of this press by a University of Rochester group, as reported in Volume 24, No. 2 of the *Journal of Clinical Investigation,* dated March 1945. This group crushed more than 400 dogs in a Blalock press in a study of the effects and causes of shock.

In all cases, the Rochester experimenters anesthetized the dog before pressure of 2,000 pounds per square inch was applied to the dog's leg. Each dog remained in the press for several hours and "in no case" was any anesthetic given during the last hour in the press. Nor was any anesthesia or sedative given later, while the dog lived.

The dogs usually died, in extreme pain, in from five to twelve hours after being released from the press, but some dogs survived the ordeal for 24 hours. Dogs —fully conscious—were tied down on a table for twelve hours after being taken out of the press. And I must repeat, none was given any drug to relieve pain.

In a study of medical periodicals a research team of the HSUS (Humane Society of the United States) has found reports of 143 other projects in which dogs were subjected to the Blalock press or to virtually identical equipment and procedures, the total number of animals used in these specific experiments being more than 4,000. Our research of the literature was by no means exhaustive.

There are various other ways of sending a dog into the kind of shock that is the result of injury and pain, and Columbia University is credited with one of the variations. There the dogs, lightly anesthetized so that the sense of pain was not eliminated, were beaten on the hind legs with a rawhide mallet. A thousand blows per leg was the average.

The Noble-Collip drum also produces shock in animals, but its big advantage over the press method is quantity. Mr. Meyers told the House about this experimental aide, too:

> This other piece of equipment on the table is known as a Noble-Collip drum; it, too, has been very widely used to produce shock in animals. The procedure is described in detail in an article entitled "A Quantitative Method for the Production of Experimental Traumatic Shock Without Hemorrhage in Unanesthetized Animals," published in the *Quarterly Journal of Experimental Physiology,* 31:187-199, 1941-42.
>
> The experimenter—if indeed this procedure can still be called experimental after many repetitions—customarily tapes together the forefeet and the hindfeet of a rat or guinea pig and places the helpless, unanesthetized animal in the drum. A door is then closed over the front of the drum and the drum is then revolved by a small electric motor at a rate of about 200 revolutions per minute. The imprisoned animal is carried nearly to the top of the wheel by centrifugal force and then is dropped by gravity to the bottom. The steel projections within the wheel insure that the animal will be sufficiently injured.
>
> Animals subjected to this procedure ultimately become unconscious in the wheel, but most of them regain consciousness for a time after removal. Like the products of the Blalock press and the rawhide ham-

mer, they live several conscious hours before they die in pain.

To date, hundreds of thousands of dogs and cats and other small animals have been tossed about in the Noble-Collip drum and one can't be blamed for wondering if medical research will ever reach a conclusion concerning shock.

The press and the drum are still with us, still grinding out torture and death to animals every year. There is no law that says they can't be used. Indeed, lawmakers, through grants, continue to subsidize their use. The House found the defense of their use both reasonable and rational. A sample of the defense: "Science has not yet proved that animals suffer. To think they suffer is anthropomorphism. We believe that any reflex or reaction is instinct and is not induced by a sensation of pain."

So the laboratory animals, in the grips of man's endless devices, continue to scream out their "instincts" and continue to die.

And we have so far had but a beginner's look at the ordeal of the animals in the United States.

Laboratory Road 2

He may not know that he's among the more fortunate, but the average stolen animal is lucky if he reaches his ultimate destination in a reasonable state of health. Care and treatment along the road to the laboratory is usually as shocking as care and treatment at the laboratory.

America's laboratories have been spending in the neighborhood of fifty million dollars per annum for stolen pets alone. Cash on the barrelhead and no questions asked are the sales terms. The seller, or animal dealer, employs the same terms with his suppliers, also known as thieves. The thieves sell by the head or by the pound. Sex, age, breed and quality of the animals are unimportant factors and do not affect the going rates.

The thieves operate from coast to coast, although in recent years they have stepped up their activities in certain states: West Virginia, New York, New Jersey, Virginia, Maryland, Ohio, North Carolina, California, Utah and Florida. Offhand, it would seem that pet owners in those states are more careless concerning supervision, but that's not the case. The thieves think nothing of invading the yards and homes of private owners, and kennels, large and small, are also considered fine hunting grounds. The popularity of the named states is based on business logic: all are within convenient driving distance to some of the nation's biggest animal dealers.

Thus, the trucks roaring down the highways do not always carry the cargoes their outside signs proclaim. Instead of poultry or furniture or groceries, the truck may well be jammed with stolen cats and dogs. And for many of the captives, the truck has been home for several days. A waterless, foodless, lightless home, the air reeking with the stench of their own excrement. It usually takes a few days for even the most accomplished thieves to collect a full load.

Then it's on to the animal dealer's "farm," the collection point from whence—tomorrow or next week, if they are still alive—they will be shipped to the laboratories. At the average farm, the pets wait their next move in filthy, overcrowded pens. Water may or may not be available. If they are fed, the rations are scanty. If the farm has had trouble with neighbors or humane society investigators, the whole load may undergo crude surgery for the removal of vocal cords. Dealers prefer to run quiet farms, and many laboratories prefer to buy quiet animals.

Those who wonder if there's money to be made in dogs and cats need look no further than the animal dealers. One of the most active in sales to laboratories enjoys an income of over three quarters of a million dollars a year. Federal agencies are among the biggest buyers.

"The business of supplying animals to laboratories is tremendously profitable and it is a real gold mine for thieves, who can sell stolen dogs for as much as ten dollars each, no questions asked," reads a report (1963) of The Humane Society of the United States. In the same year, a special United States Senate Commission predicted that by 1970 the monetary value of animals used annually in laboratories would equal the value of all livestock produced by American farms and ranches.

In this respect, 1970 is already here. That's why dealers' farms continue to flourish and why the curve on stolen pets is ever upward. A clean, sanitary, humane farm is rare, and it has been difficult to put substandard farms out of business. If actual proof of cruelty to animals can be obtained, and if local or state laws exist, and if local authorities can be stirred to the boiling point, then a conviction is possible. But even then the dealer just pays his small fine—for a misdemeanor, not a felony—and goes right back into business, either at his old stand or a new one. And it is seemingly impossible to nail a dealer on his traffic in stolen animals. Where are the real owners?

And always, there are the dealers' laboratory connections. The smart ones insure themselves against occasional trouble by doing a little boarding on the side. For one reason or another, lack of room or insufficient staff, for instance, laboratories do board some of their animals at farms. Almost always these animals have been through one research ordeal and need time to recuperate before facing another.

That was the precise case in New York State. By some miracle, a team of humane society investigators, including one veterinarian, gained access to an animal dealer's farm. Of the hundreds of dogs present, the majority were convalescing from major surgery. Old farm buildings were the hospitals, and the convalescent wards were filthy overcrowded pens. Dogs with open chest wounds and badly infected incisions, so weak that many could not stand, were the order of the day. These dogs were "recuperating" from open-heart and kidney surgery. A litter of two-day-old pups were found in a basket, with no food provisions in sight. A bitch in her last hours of pregnancy, bleeding from lacerations received in a dogfight, was found in a pen with fifty other dogs. In every pen there were dogs suffering from contagious diseases.

To the investigators, it seemed like an open and shut case. But in New York and other states, licensed laboratories are immune from ordinary anticruelty laws, and these boarding convalescents were owned by state universities, city hospitals, and the United States Public Health Service. Furthermore, the farm had been inspected several times by the state's own department of health, and it had been found "clean and suitable." End of case.

The smart dealer is always prepared for intruders and can wave a fistful of legitimate bills of sale. While thieves are important suppliers, he can't always depend on them for quantity or variety. So he has his own collection trucks rolling through the countryside, visiting rural and backwoods points on schedule. The local people don't know him, but they know that his truck will be parked behind the old hotel opposite the courthouse on the third Tuesday of the month. The truck's driver will buy almost anything—dogs, pups, cats, kittens, rabbits, hamsters, pigeons, chickens—all at pennies per pound. The poorer the community, the faster the truck loads.

Another cheap source of supply is the animal auction. It may be news to city people, but these auctions are weekly events in many rural areas. The animals arrive in boxes, crates, sacks and bags and are dumped into holding pens until ready for the gavel. An obviously purebred dog may bring ten dollars, or a few dollars more if he's accompanied by falsified registration papers. A litter of mongrel pups may bring a dollar. At these auctions, a dealer has no trouble replenishing his supply at economy rates. And sometimes he finds the auction a great place to unload his overstock. It's always cheaper to sell than to feed.

The dealers seldom seem to be worried about overstock, however. Sooner or later, an order will come from a laboratory, and that's where the dollars are. Meanwhile, if the dealer holds on to enough of everything, enough will survive to fill the order. A look at humane society reports from just a few states tells the whole, nauseating story:

INDIANA: "Animals were crowded in small wire cages, with wire bottoms. Cages were stacked in tiers, with urine and feces from upper cages dripping on animals in lower units." Of added interest is the fact that the dealer's brother, a veterinarian, was drawing blood from the caged dogs to fulfill his own orders from one of the nation's leading pharmaceutical companies.

PENNSYLVANIA: "It was a chamber of horrors. The stench alone was enough to tell the story," this referring to 4,000 rabbits crowded into small cages that had never been cleaned. The rabbits were in a barn along with 400 cats stuffed in poultry crates stacked six feet high. Eight or nine cats were in each crate, some with deadly feline enteritis, and others already dead. In other buildings on the premises were several thousand pigeons, hamsters, guinea pigs, white rats and mice. Six hundred dogs jammed one building, with fifty and more crowded into each ten-by-ten-foot wire-covered pen. Three truckloads of dogs arrived while the investigation was in progress. Puppies examined were running high temperatures, many dogs carried distemper, the strong walked on top of the weak. No provisions were made for the sick or injured animals. The little food available was green with mold and none of the hungry animals was eating it.

Despite the evidence, this particular animal dealer's farm must be considered one of the finest in the land. To understand this remark, one must consult the directory published by the National Academy of Science and the National Research Council, and based upon information supplied by the Institute of Laboratory Animal Resources, which operates under Public Service Grant #GM-03991, courtesy of America's taxpayers. The directory's foreword states: "In the area of animal quality, the Institute has developed standards for the production, care, maintenance, shipment and utilization of experimental animals." The farm in question is listed and met those standards.

Too often, the Federal Government pops up as an accessory to the animal farm problem. A typical case occurred in Tennessee, where humane society investigators and local law officers visited a small farm and found conditions so deplorable that the dealer was charged immediately with cruelty to animals. Live dogs were penned with dead and badly decomposed ones, to name just one of the pieces of evidence. The dealer confessed that he bought and caught up to 200 stray dogs a week and sold the still-living by the pound to a kennel in Pennsylvania. The kennel turned out to be another farm and one of the largest animal suppliers to the National Institutes of Health.

If the dealers gave free, guided tours of their farms to the general public, only the insane among us would sleep well at night. As it is, the average citizen can't even buy his way onto one of the farms, and humane society agents are the least welcome of all. Still, the agents do manage to get around, and they do make reports. If the reports sound similar, that's because animal farms are similar. The following conditions, all gleaned from reports, have been observed in animal farms throughout the nation:

Dam trying to nurse litter of dead pups, rooster with leg hanging by thread of skin, decayed ducks, sick and starving sheep, half-eaten dogs and rabbits, variety of animals with open chest wounds, the still-living penned with the dead, occupied cages stacked in the broiling sun, drinking water black and full of garbage, rats eating a mother cat and her kittens, pups jammed into chicken crates, ponies too weak to stand, emaciated monkeys, rabbits with moldy coats, starving pigeons, intense stench, dog and cat fights, piles of dead animals, overcrowding everywhere, pens and sheds and barns that have never been cleaned, a thousand guinea pigs occupying sixteen square feet of floor space, goat dragging broken leg, debeaked geese, sore-covered calves, general filth, rotted food, variety of diseased animals, dung so high that donkey can't stand in stall, hamsters eating dead dog, white mice dining on dying white mice, and a never-ending chorus of moans from the dying, suffering, starving, bewildered representatives of the animal kingdom.

So a given animal's road to a laboratory is seldom a direct one. Whether he's stolen, picked up as a stray, or purchased, there's a detour first to the animal dealer's farm. There he waits—never under satisfactory conditions—until his ride to his journey's end.

One of the miracles of our form of government is that prolonged shouting and ample proof can sometimes stir our lawmakers. If a sufficient number of organizations and private citizens shout loudly enough and long enough, and, if they can find and haul tons of evidence to Washington, Congress will sometimes move. That's just what happened in 1966, the year Congress passed the Laboratory Animal Welfare Act (PL-89-544), a bill designed to guarantee at least minimum standards of care for the animals to be used in medical research, and to cure the abuses at the animal farm level. The Act became a law in August of 1966, and is now enforceable by the Department of Agriculture. It is to be hoped that the rigid enforcement of this Act will remedy many of the conditions discussed in these pages.

The animal dealers are not worried. Only 300,000 dollars were appropriated for the new law. Just enough to license dealers, and for routine inspection. As things stand now, a dealer in laboratory animals might obtain a license by certifying that he meets the minimum standards. If the Government can't afford to inspect his farm, the law is a joke, and only the abused animals aren't laughing.

Nobody can realistically argue against the use of animals in research. The lower animals have always served the highest one and always will, as meat for the table, for instance, no matter how vegetarians feel. And certainly much of medical science would still be back in the dark ages if researchers had not used animals in their work.

But one can argue against needless abuses in the laboratories. Federal, state, city, or university—they are all licensed, and they all provide their own supervision. In varying degrees, all are supported by the taxpayers' dollars. And all are immune from existing anti-cruelty laws, because of other laws that say that's the case. Such as the section under the Penal Code of the

State of California which says, "No part of this title shall be construed as interfering with any of the laws of this state known as the 'game laws' or any laws for or against the destruction of certain birds, . . . or with properly conducted scientific experiments or investigations performed under the authority of the faculty of a regularly incorporated medical college or university of this state" (Pen. 599c). Such exceptions are typical.

So the laboratories have the public's trust and the public's dollars. If those who work within their walls regard them as sacred institutions, there's nothing wrong with that attitude. Their work is for the benefit of mankind. But what they don't seem to understand is that the public's trust, not to mention money, is based upon the assumption that they, the scientists and medical researchers, will demonstrate a little compassion for their animal charges.

Even the layman understands that it is necessary for the animals to be conscious and unanesthetized during certain experiments, no matter the agony of the subjects. And that it is sometimes necessary to use ten or a hundred or a thousand animals to prove a point, and to repeat the test until positive proof is assured.

But once the point has been established, is it really necessary for scores of other laboratories and new researchers to repeat the test and waste tens of thousands of lives just to verify what is already known? Isn't there a saturation point? The public's trust is in medical research, not in superfluous medical research.

They're busy in the laboratories, but not too busy to be aware of needless repetitions. And while one may grant them ignorance of what goes on at the animal farms, surely some of them must be aware of conditions on their own premises.

One who was aware and disturbed about them was a scientist with the Food and Drug Administration. Shocked by the living conditions of the FDA's experimental animals, he leaked word to Ann Cottrell Free of the North American Newspaper Alliance. Her report:

"In those windowless, sub-basement rooms, hundreds of dogs flung themselves against the bars of their cages, piled tier on tier. They were barking, screaming, and whining. A few were mute and dropped their heads in the dark corners. Others circled ceaselessly in their cages. The steel grids beneath their feet showed their pathetic, circular path. These dogs, mostly beagles, are used primarily for the testing of food additives. Some remain in their cages seven years."

It's possible that the FDA leaders had forgotten all about the dogs in the subbasement, for they were very busy planning a new, 26-million-dollar office and laboratory building. So Mrs. Free checked into the plans and discovered that the FDA—despite her recent article and the great wave of criticism it had provoked—intended to cage its dogs in the usual manner and was making no provision for exercise of any kind. It took four years of crusading before the FDA relented and provided more suitable quarters for its 500 dogs.

Still, this was just one case, and students of laboratory techniques took it in stride. After all, this was only a matter of 500 dogs, whereas in other laboratories thousands of animals are living in conditions fully as bad or worse than those of the animal dealers' farms: stacked in cages and crates, including the diseased, the dying and the dead. Indeed, in some cages the living walk over the dead, if they have room to move at all. Dogs used in surgery practice techniques stand around with open chest wounds and badly infected incisions. Mother dogs and their pups are trampled. The stench of accumulated filth is often overwhelming. Feces and urine drip down from the top cages through the stacked cages to the bottom one. Cleaning is not too much of a problem: an attendant hoses out the quarters with the animals still inside. Sometimes, it's the only fresh water the animals get. They lick the water on the filthy floor.

All this shouldn't be news, although it probably is. The shocking facts were published in book form by the HSUS. Disturbed by rumors of laboratory conditions and thwarted in all attempts to hold open investigations, the society hatched a long-range plan that was designed to circumvent all obstacles and reveal the whole truth. Viewed as a plot, the plan was a masterpiece of spy fiction. A small army of special investigators was hired and then trained in basic laboratory techniques. Thus qualified, the investigators fanned out and found employment in the nation's leading laboratories. The daily, on-the-scene reports that soon flooded back to the society confirmed even the worst rumors of inhumane confinement, neglect of animals during periods of postexperimental pain, and repetitious torture of animals for no apparent research objective.

For over fifteen years now, humanitarians and other interested groups have been urging legislation to guarantee, at the very least, decent living conditions and proper care for the experimental animals while they await, or recover from, their day in research. But the laboratory authorities fight even this simple control. They argue that it would cause too much paper work, and thus impede the progress of medical science. They assure Congress that laboratory animals are treated like pampered pets. It is as if they believe that all documents are false and all photographs lie. Indeed, some who claim to know the canine mind better than others insist that a dog is happy to be kept inside a small cage for five or seven years, and that such a happy dog does not need exercise. But wait—is happiness an instinct? Whatever happened to anthropomorphism?

There are those who argue that the noble Laboratory Animal Welfare Act could be the answer to the dilemma, if only sufficient funds were made available. Then, at least in laboratories operating under federal grants, the Department of Agriculture could police. It would help, but it would be similar to a policeman checking on a policeman, for the billion-a-year in federal grants is the responsibility of the National Institutes of Health.

This arm of the Government conducts its own vast

program of experimentation on animals with one hand, and with the other it hands over funds to research laboratories in this country and abroad. Unfortunately, the NIH is too busy to police its favorite laboratories, and sometimes it finances the oddest research.

To the tune of $51,000, it underwrote a three-year study of sleep deprivation. In this endurance test, the animals were required to run for 23 hours, rest for a single hour, then run for 23 more. During the hour off the running wheel, a pistol was shot off to disturb the resters. The experiment was a repetition of others conducted in 1927, 1929 and 1946.

Then there's the NIH grant of $160,000 to a university interested in discovering what happens when electric shock is applied to tooth pulp. This has been a favorite with researchers since 1938, and all seem happy to do it again at the drop of a federal grant, even though the results have been established. The project calls for deep holes to be drilled in the subject's canine teeth, so deep that the pulp (nerve) can be seen. Electrodes are cemented into all of the holes, and wires are run (under the skin) from the electrodes to the top of the animal's head. The fully conscious animal is placed in a restraining harness and the electrodes are stimulated. The trick is to determine which one of his teeth hurt him the most. This single tooth is then used for the balance of the experiment. How does the animal react to the pain when he's given morphine? What's his reaction to the toothache when he's on nalorphine? The reactions are always the same. All of those tax dollars can't change the results.

If one Canadian scientist isn't on the verge of curing all the world's ills, don't blame the NIH. Thus far, it's granted him at least $785,000, other federal agencies have chipped in another $345,000, and the end of the study is not in sight. This project has been going on for thirteen years, and the suffering of animals is important to it. Among the groups that would like to have a clear idea of the intended goal is the National Catholic Society for Animal Welfare, which has been wondering about the NIH itself for more than thirteen years: "Much of the NIH-supported experimentation is a duplication or repetition of work already performed or in progress. Researchers are under no compulsion . . . to determine whether experiments they are performing have already been performed, often repeatedly. This means that they may inflict the same suffering on animals that other researchers have already inflicted, often repetitiously." Obviously, the NIH has never felt compelled to double-check, either. It can be presumed that the NIH has never heard of the Science Information Exchange, a fine clearinghouse for such matters.

"The end justifies the means" is the theme song of the laboratories, and it may have been composed in the halls of the tax-wealthy NIH. Nobody is arguing.

But of course new experiments are also being performed, and these days the big emphasis is on the fields of drugs and chemicals. As the new drug and chemical formulas come along, they fall into the custody of the Food and Drug Administration. The new drug that doesn't meet the FDA standards of safety does not reach the marketplace. Animals are used for the testing, but here also the use of animals is often senseless, for their reactions prove nothing of value to man.

As the American Medical Association put it at a congressional hearing:

> Drug activity in animals is no assurance of similar activity in humans, and for some human disorders there are no similar disorders in animals. Frequently, animal studies prove little or nothing and are very difficult to correlate to humans. In some instances, expensive animal studies are not indicated because there is no likelihood of their providing worthwhile, realistic evidence to the sponsor and clinical investigators. In most instances, the proper formula, dosage form and dosage level can only be determined by clinical trials on human beings.

And as a drug-company executive said: "Animal studies are done for legal reasons and not for scientific reasons. The predictive value of such studies for man is often meaningless . . . which means our research may be meaningless."

Under FDA regulations, testing of new drugs is the same today as it was years ago. The first step of the "toxicity testing" requires using four species of animals.

They are run through a series of acute poisoning tests, and at least half, but not all, must die. If this is not the case, then the drug's potency is improved and the tests are rerun until at least half of the animals die. When that happens, the tissues of the dead animals are examined and the next step is at hand. This requires two species of animals, and they are run through a series of subacute poisoning tests. These are known as tolerance tests. They last for two weeks, and the object is twofold: how much of the drug can the animals take without dying, and how little of the drug can they take without discernible effect? The tissues of all, the living and the dead, are examined. It is at this point that the safe human dose is calculated. Now a third group of animals is put on a diet of drug-dosed food. Since the animals reject the food, tube-feeding is usually required, and if the drug affects them adversely, the adverse effects are then studied, although nobody is sure whether they were caused by the drug or malnutrition.

The scientific and technological worlds have made huge strides in the past ten years, and only the FDA fails to recognize the fact that living animals are not reliable subjects for the testing of drugs. Thanks to the development of high-powered microscopes and new knowledge, such insentient materials as tissue cultures and cells are superior in terms of economy, efficiency and results. And now we know that in many experiments utilizing vertebrates, invertebrates can be substituted and achieve the same results.

Waste in government is one thing; it seems to be an accepted liability of democracy. But the wasting of lives is something else.

How did we ever get this way?

Start 'em Young 3

Irreverence for life begins best at an early age. If it doesn't occur naturally, then our system of education, public and private, serves as a remedy.

Each year, millions of American high-school students learn through observation that a frog's heart will beat long after the frog himself is dead. A frog is mounted on one board, his heart is removed and mounted on another board, and the students watch as the frog dies and his heart beats on and on. This simple experiment proves to the boys and girls that teacher is absolutely right when he says, "You can't live very long when disassociated from your heart, even if the heart keeps beating."

It is the beginning of nightmares for some students, and is probably the reason why many mature women shudder when they note frog's legs on the menu. They remember when they were teen-agers in biology class.

Why aren't all species of frogs now extinct? The frog is a prolific breeder, for one thing. So are the rat and the rabbit, two favorites of junior high-school teachers.

At this junior level, American boys and girls are ready to learn that proper diet results in a healthy body, whereas improper diet causes difficulties and no diet at all means starvation and death. To illustrate, three healthy rabbits are placed in separate cages. One is fed a proper diet, Two is fed an improper diet, and Three isn't fed at all. This goes on for weeks, or until the children can see for themselves that One is as healthy as ever, Two's teeth are falling out, and Three is dead. It can be presumed that the children are now properly conditioned for high school and the frog.

There are other, better, humane ways to teach the basic facts of life to youngsters, but educators seem to feel that needless cruelty is the best method of all. The teachers see nothing wrong in the experiments. They were exposed to similar experiments in their youth, and now they are simply following the manual and doing their duty.

A favorite joke with science teachers is "My landlady says her cat is missing." What it means is that on Friday the teacher told several of his promising students to find some cats and bring them in on Monday for classroom work. By the time the joke is told, the landlady's cat and the other stolen pets have been properly dissected and their organs occupy various jars.

Calling upon students to supply the animals to be used in classroom work is common practice. The students are not about to bring in their own pets, of course, and the teachers know that they are in effect asking the student to steal.

The stealing of cats or anything else does not belong in a school's curriculum, and it proved to be the last straw for a group of irate parents in one eastern community last year. They were unhappy with the biology teacher anyway, for he had turned his class into a chamber of horrors. When he ordered his students to steal a few cats, it was too much for the parents, who marched on the office of the school superintendent. He listened to their complaints: they didn't want their children to be sadists, they didn't want their children to be thieves. "Please understand," said the school superintendent. "We have to keep up with the Russians."

It's possible that our youngsters have already overtaken Russia's. Here, at any rate, science-thrilled and class-inspired youngsters are carrying on their own experiments in kitchens, basements and garages. Without supervision, they are injecting drugs and stimulants into the veins of animals, carrying out crude surgery, inducing cancer in animals, implanting electrodes, and shooting rodents into the sky.

In a sense, they cannot be blamed, for they find encouragement almost everywhere. For many, the highlight of the school year is the local science fair, where the winning displays too often feature animal abuse. And it's a rare school library that doesn't contain material—published at the taxpayer's expense—encouraging projects for students which feature the suffering of animals.

One of many examples is the *Science Projects Handbook*, supplied to schools by the National Science Foundation, itself tax-supported. "Nearly a million teen-age boys and girls throughout the world are having fun discovering science," is the handbook's modest claim. All sorts of fun, such as placing pregnant rats and mice in a refrigerator so that the resultant newborns will be monstrosities. Out of seventeen mice born of such an experiment, one had a skinless skull, one a malpositi[illegible] heart, two had malpositioned testes, and two had blood tumors of the brain.

How many children are shooting for a better record? Or entertaining themselves with another experiment, with instructions for producing cancer in baby chicks and turkeys? Or having even more fun by tracing the progress of the cancer through the body of the growing bird?

The handbook doesn't promise it, but it's possible for the funsters to gain fame. An Ohio high-school student did just that by sewing windows into the abdomens of three white, pregnant rats, then watching the development of the babies. With instruments borrowed from a friendly veterinarian, the young man, ably assisted by his mother, ended the lives of all the rats, young and old. For all this he won a prize, a glowing article in the local paper, and the envy of his schoolmates.

Every day of the week, the local press reports similar lunacies, thus encouraging more youngsters to experiment at home and inflict more pain on animals for no reason at all. This may please the educators, and presumably it worries Russia.

Some voices of protest have been heard, but the most effective voice of all, the National Congress of Parents and Teachers, has been strangely silent. The late Eleanor Roosevelt tried to stir it into action many years ago:

"It seems to me of great importance to teach our children respect for life. Toward this end, experiments on living animals in classrooms should be stopped. To encourage cruelty—in the name of science—can only destroy the finer emotions of affection and sympathy and breed an unfeeling callousness toward suffering in all living creatures."

Her words did not disturb the conscience of the NCPT. Nor did this sort of frontal attack from the News Analysis Group of Everett, Washington:

> At enormous expense to the taxpayers, the school children of America are being carefully trained in delinquency. We make the accusation in sober earnest, and with great concern for the future.
>
> Under the guise of "scientific research," an increasing number of schools, even the elementary schools, are adopting programs of experimentation on living animals. From the comparatively mild "dietary project," wherein small animals are deprived of food elements necessary to their growth and well being, as an "object lesson" in unwise eating habits, to the inexpressibly sadistic dissection of living animals—at times only partially anesthetized—the nefarious program is accepted into school curriculum after curriculum. If an occasional alarmed parent should protest, it is without avail.
>
> Instructors agree that the average child is shocked and sickened by these "projects" at first, but they announce with satisfaction that this same child soon becomes "avid" in pursuing the subject. At their most impressionable age, to be subjected to a course of training which is represented to them as being approved by the most highly respected authority, derided by their fellows as "chicken," normal children learn to suppress their loathing and conform to the routine demanded

> by their instructors. Soon, very soon, these naturally well disposed little ones become the potential "delinquents" who provide our medium with the ever increasing flood of "teen-age" crimes. Some are found torturing dogs and cats; some, since it is but a short step from the "experiment" on a four-footed animal to the human species, adopt a career of murder, rape, arson, and other unspeakable crimes.
>
> What, in God's name, are the Parent Teachers Associations doing to safeguard the mental and moral health of the Citizens of Tomorrow? Such pseudo-scientific programs add nothing to the store of scientific knowledge. Results of each "experiment" are already well established, TOO WELL ESTABLISHED! With our money and with our children, then, our public schools are training delinquents.
>
> The schools do not belong to the teachers and the school officials, but to the parents. And so do the children.

Those words may have been written in anger, but they still contain gold. Ever since juvenile delinquency became a tidal wave, educators have been pointing their fingers at parents. Society knows, or thinks it knows, that the trouble begins at home. The parents just don't know how to bring up a child in proper fashion. Thus the parents, not the children, are the true delinquents.

It's high time for parents to admit their guilt, but in terms of mistaken identity. Let them point their fingers at the educators. Parents have been delinquent in not knowing or caring about what's been going on in our schools.

They have the power to change things. In every

state, the overseer of all public schools is the state board of education. In turn, this state body pays homage to its state's educational code. In effect, the state code is the state's law concerning public schools, for it was voted upon and approved by the state's legislature. Somewhere in the codes, the purposes of teaching are outlined. Morality, truth, justice and patriotism are common to all, and most include the humane treatment of animals. Most parents are unaware of such codes. So, apparently, are most science teachers.

Also unaware are the editors of the National Science Teachers Association, who published an article by a high-school biology teacher concerning his astonishing triumphs in the classroom. He and his students had successfully produced cancer in live animals, achieved "violent shutting off of the glottis" by blowing smoke into the lungs of live mice, and implanted an artificial heart with apparatus designed by a schoolgirl. His enthusiastic students even took animals home for experiments of an original nature. But he was proudest of his personal, psychological technique for eliminating "squeamishness" in children. This amounted to forbidding the students to give names to the animals. "It is too easy to become emotionally attached," the teacher explained, "and thus become strongly disturbed at seeing a friend handled directly."

Apart from "keeping up with the Russians," the educators have offered very little defense for the mayhem that goes on in the classrooms. When it comes, it is often of an ivory tower nature, such as this from a noted college biology professor: "It is true that a few children may be harmed by witnessing or participating in this so-called cruelty, but this harm could be far outweighed by the production of *only one* great medical researcher." Is it possible that he had a particular experiment in mind? The one devised by an imaginative high-school teacher (Oak Park, Illinois), wherein a rat was fed an exclusive diet of bourbon whiskey, then killed (after four months) in the hopes of finding evidence of cirrhosis of the liver? Will the great one come from that biology class?

Fortunately, most college-level thinking is on the side of humanitarians and parents.

From Harvard:

> Education is not merely in the imparting of knowledge, but the cultivation of certain aptitudes and attitudes in the minds of the young. The objective of knowledge is not just knowledge of values, but commitment to them. . . . To isolate the activity of thinking from the morals of thinking is to make sophists of the young.

Florida agrees. At the adult level, as future pages will reveal, its lawmakers do not work too strenuously to avoid cruelty to animals. But it is a model for all other states at the juvenile level, and its Department of Education is the first such body thus far to issue an anti-cruelty guide for secondary-school science teachers:

> In many cases, animals should be kept in biology classrooms so that students can be given opportunities to

be trained in careful observation of animal behavior. This is important if students are to learn effectively the many facts about animal behavior, heredity, learning ability, natural habitats, sociological factors, adequate care as related to eating, sleeping, exercising, compatibility with other animals or those of like kind but of the same or different sex.

A science teacher who proposes to use live animals in teaching procedures must be aware, first of all, that issues of morality may be and often are involved. It is important that the health and well-being of animals not be interfered with when they are being used in the classroom.

The teacher must also realize that any classroom use of animals, even those that by most persons would be regarded as benign, may evoke disturbing emotional reactions in some students. Demonstrations or experiments in which animals are unnecessarily killed or are subjected to any procedure that offends a student's moral and ethical standards may, in the opinion of many psychologists and psychiatrists, be harmfully traumatic to the student. A student may "learn" many things from classroom use of animals, and physiology may be the least of them.

When animals are used as teaching aids in the classroom, it is suggested that these recommendations be followed:

1. Do not kill animals in the presence of students.
2. Animals shall be kept in the classroom for the minimum time necessary for the teaching purpose. If kept over weekends or during holidays, a responsible person shall provide daily food and water and shall clean the cages.

3. All animals must at all times have a plentiful supply of fresh, clean water and healthful food, appropriate to the species.
4. Cages and enclosures for animals shall be appropriate to the species and the number of animals, allowing room for healthful exercise and comfortable existence, with provision for humane environmental conditions—temperature, humidity, and the like.
5. It should be emphasized to students that cruelty to animals is unethical and in Florida is illegal.
6. The teacher using animals in a classroom is personally responsible for maintaining these standards and for carefully considering the ethical and moral issues involved.

It's a pity that we can't turn the clock back. The ordeal of the animals would be lessened if all of today's animal dealers and laboratory directors were young again and going to school in Florida.

There's not much interest in the other 49 states. It's as if parents put all their trust in teachers, and teachers trust all superintendents, and superintendents never question their state director, and he in turn has mislaid or forgotten or never heard of his state's education code. And what about the local school board? Does everybody outside of Florida believe that child psychology amounts to two words and nothing more?

These words, purloined from Dr. James T. Mehorter, are solemnly dedicated to all of the above:

> We need to strive to develop in youngsters such personality traits as empathy and compassion in order to help them develop a humanely oriented philosophy

> of life and make a successful personal adjustment. We need to provide youngsters with experiences that conduce positively toward the development of humane feeling, thought and action toward all sentient life. . . . Society today is in large measure characterized by an over-abundance of anxiety, a pervasive tension or stress manifesting itself in terms of aggressiveness, selfishness, and other types of unkindly behaviors. Increasingly, I am persuaded, there is a tendency in the school to "condition"—educate is a misnomer—condition the pupil to "adjust" to this social reality, and I'm rather concerned because this reality tends to be endowed with such disintegrative emotional patterns as jealousy, distrust, hostility, prejudice and unkindness. The integrative emotions of love, joy, empathy, affection, compassion and kindness—the psychologically healthful traits of personality and culture—tend to have been eclipsed and play relatively minor roles in the human affairs of contemporary reality.

As President Johnson said, "We are determined that compassion shall not pass from the nation's soul."

All thinking Americans agreed, and even high-school biology teachers applauded his remark as they prepared the next day's lesson, on how to prove that a cat doesn't really have nine lives.

The Wild West 4

Our national indifference to animal cruelty at home does not prevent us from being highly critical of practices in other lands. Many Americans, including medical researchers and biology teachers, disapprove of bullfighting, and rightly so. Even our lawmakers are against bullfighting, and every state—almost every state—has seen to it that nobody breaks the law.

This doesn't mean that bullfighting won't reach our shores. Laws can be changed, and the pressure to legalize bullfighting grows every day. And make no mistake about it, if this sort of slaughter can be legalized, every seat in every stadium will be filled. No matter what they've heard about it, the curious will flock to see anything new, and there are other millions of Americans who just can't wait, those who, as tourists, witnessed fights abroad and found them thrilling spectacles. The average tourist, unfortunately, doesn't understand all that he's seeing in the ring. Either that, or he's read too much Hemingway. And then there are the millions whose appetites have been whetted by films and television. They are innocent, too.

Television is already doing a good job of conditioning the American public to what may come. One of the most popular world reference books in school libraries refers to the bullfight as "a contest in which men fight against maddened bulls," and then goes on to give a superficial explanation of the action. The matador emerges as a hero, there's no mention of the cruelties, and no word about blood.

And Houston's huge Astrodome has already been home to a "bloodless bullfight," a new term that enabled the promoters to skirt the law, stage the show and reap enormous profits. The bulls wore protective shields (of paper, not metal) and everybody knew beforehand that the shields were a sham. The Governor wouldn't intervene, for the Texas law that prohibits bullfights doesn't mention bloodless bullfights. So the show went on as advertised, tens of thousands watched, and only the blind missed seeing the blood-soaked shields that had not protected the bulls, and the blood oozing from the sides of horses ripped by the sharp rowels of Mexican spurs. Investigators were on hand to seize the bloody evidence, so that the same deceit couldn't be staged again. They presented the proof that it had not been a bloodless affair, but Houston preferred to look the other way. The judge had been there, and he found the event an exhibition of "skill, daring, and grace." Civic authorities found the event "gratifying." So did the promoters.

One of the few protesting voices was that of a visiting New Yorker, the late Bill Slocum:

> No matter what kind of an animal is chased into the arena, the end result will be the same. He will be tormented, teased and tortured, all toward the noble end of gate receipts. And if he is not tormented, teased and tortured, there won't be any gate receipts. . . . The

> very word bullfight is a sham. A bullfight is not a fight between a bull and a man; it is a fight between one dumb bull and a gang of smart armed men. If bullfighting is a fight, then eight guys mugging a helpless drunk is a sporting contest.

To date, attempts to introduce bloodless bullfighting to other states haven't been successful. Unlike Texas, those other states found that their existing anticruelty laws were sufficient to forbid the spectacles. But the promoters are still in there trying, for there's big money to be made in bloodless bullfights, and the bloodless affairs would condition the public for the real thing, where the huge money is.

The promoters are patient, generous men. In New Orleans they offered a large donation to the American Humane Association on the condition that objections to bullfighting be withdrawn. Disappointed but not really discouraged, the bold ones still seek a breakthrough in Louisiana, one of two states that they regard as the promised land. The other is California, whose San Diego County realizes some 250 million dollars per annum from a daily average of over 72,000 tourists. The big tourist attraction is bullfighting, but it takes place just across the border in nearby Mexico. So the tourists spend even more of their time and money in Mexico, and wouldn't it be nice if they spent all of their time and all of their money in San Diego County? This dream of many a local merchant would become reality if bullfighting were legalized in California. Wouldn't this keep the American traveler and his dollars at home? Isn't this consistent with President Johnson's pleas to see America first? So what's wrong with bullfighting? Isn't there fun to be had in viewing a slaughterhouse?

If anything can be more degrading and demoralizing than the sights of the slaughterhouse, surely it is the bullfight, the deliberate, prolonged torture of a single animal. Under the guise of pageantry, a small army of specialists apply the tools of their trade, and each tool is a gift of more pain to the bull. Finally, after twenty minutes or so—when he has lost enough blood, when his neck muscles have been so damaged that he can hook to neither the right nor left, when his strength is gone and only the anger induced by his multiple pains keeps him going—the bull is judged ready to meet the fearless matador. By this time, if the specialists have not been careless, the dying bull can do no more than charge in a straight line. So the matador plays with the bull, goads him, and finally kills him. It is a mercy killing in the sense that the bull is going to die anyway.

On a sunny afternoon in Spain (or Mexico, or Portugal), six bulls, each bred and carefully raised for just this day, enter the ring under their own power and later are dragged from the ring as dead, bloody hulks. They go to their sure dooms one at a time, of course, and the beginning of the end for each starts with a meat hook implanted in his shoulders. This is known as the divisa, and the ribbons attached to it represent the bull's ranch. The divisa is regarded as an honor, but this "honor" hurts the bull and infuriates him. It is the least of his tortures. Next come the pics (five-inch steel spikes) and then the banderillas (five-inch steel barbs), all carefully planted to assure the damage of muscles, a steady flow of blood, and death in slow stages. Finally, with only his legs in reasonably good shape, he meets his master—the brave matador. This hero with a sword knows that his whole career is at stake: if he doesn't time things just right and kill the bull before it drops dead of its own accord, then he, the matador, is a bum.

The bullfight is a Spanish tradition, of course, and the Spanish see nothing wrong with it. It's not a contest, for the bull cannot win, nor can it be called "sporting," for the odds favor the man. For two centuries, the Spanish have considered it more or less adult entertainment, and in Madrid, the law forbids the attendance of children under fourteen years of age. None of them, adults or children, understand why we won't tolerate bullfights over here. They have every right to wonder about our attitude, for we have a gory tradition of our own. It's called the rodeo, and the youngest American may attend one without breaking any laws.

The rodeo bull may well envy his Spanish cousins. It's all over for them in one afternoon, but for him it's just one rodeo after another, and all of them are painful experiences.

Spectators get their first good look at the rodeo bull when the gate opens and he comes bucking into view with the apparent intent of unloading his rider. The fact is that the rider is of secondary interest to the bull. The animal is reacting to the flank or bucking strap, an invention that encircles him and pains him from the time he leaves the chute. There may be barbed wire under the bucking strap, or sharp tacks, or heavy needles, placed there to pierce the hide and flesh and to guarantee that the bull will buck. Most onlookers have never heard of a flank strap, and those who have are probably unaware that the bull, before he was driven into the chute, was beaten, whipped and goaded. The combination of fear and pain turns the bull into an exciting performer, and the wilder he reacts, the higher the fee his devoted owner can command at the next show.

A good, bucking bull, who reacts violently to pain, can look forward to a long career on the rodeo circuit. A speedy steer, on the other hand, never knows when his glory days will come to a sudden end. In one of his rodeo roles, he is chased by a mounted cowboy, roped, brought to the ground, and bound. The object of steer roping, of course, is to complete the job in record time, and even a stupid cowboy knows that an unconscious steer's legs can be tied without delay. A frightened, struggling steer, on the other hand, can kick a cowboy right out of the prize money.

In rodeo parlance, the mounted man "busts" the steer by tightening the rope and bringing the steer down. It's a very apt term, for a clever man with a rope knows just how to angle, turn, and slam the steer to the ground. Proper busting only means potential prize money for the man, but for the steer it means a variety of possibilities: wrenched horns, torn muscles, broken bones, internal injuries—or death from a broken neck.

The steer is also important in what is known as bulldogging. Again, like the bucking bull, the steer is tortured into a frenzy and then released from the chute. As he races out he's chased by a mounted cowboy. Soon the man leaps from the saddle and grabs for the steer's neck. Gripping the animal's horns, he forces the head down and sideways until a fall is achieved. In the case of a stubborn steer, it helps if the man's fingers find the sensitive nostrils and yank sideways. But stubborn or not, the steer's impact with the ground can have a fatal result.

Is the applause from the stands for the gallant man, or is it a tribute to the dead steer? For the man, of course. The announcer, as the steer's corpse is hauled away, is always careful to explain, "Don't worry, folks. The steer is okay. Just had the wind knocked out of him."

The afternoon's next event might be the saddle bronco riding, outstanding for at least two things: cowboy courage and cowboy cruelty. Backstage, the bronco receives treatment as rough as that extended to the bull and the steer. The horse is driven from the holding corral, then beaten and goaded and poked along into a chute so narrow that he cannot budge. He's confused, wild, and full of fear as the crew leans over the rails with the saddle and bucking strap, and perhaps slips under each sharp objects of torture. The older and wearier the bronco, the more preliminary pain must be administered to insure a proper show of wildness in the arena. Now saddle and cinch are firm, and the flanking strap is tightened until it cuts into the flesh of the loins. The pain is excruciating.* The rider climbs aboard; at the same moment, an electric prod may be jammed into the horse's rectum. The gate opens: horse and rider charge into view, and the rider rakes the horse with his spurs. The crowd cheers as the horse bucks. What they are cheering is the expressions of his agony.

When time is up, a pick-up rider rescues the cowboy, and in doing so, he loosens the bucking strap. The bronco stops bucking and is led away. Meanwhile, another bronco is being readied in the chute. If it's his first time out, the crew is probably joking about the distance he'll leap when he feels the hot prod in his rectum.

One would think that at least baby animals could be spared public suffering, but such is not the case. Rodeos also make use of calves. Considering the overall treatment of livestock, it's a wonder that calves aren't used in branding contests. But branding would be a little strong for the faint of heart in the audience, so the rodeo promoters have compromised and voted for roping contests.

In back of the stands, it's the same old story. Enough beating, whipping and prodding will move any calf into his assigned chute, and a hot shot in the rectum will send him flying through the gate right on schedule. Then, as the terrorized youngster gallops off in pain, a

* The inguinal and flank areas of an animal's body are highly sensitive; any device applied to them can easily cause pain and discomfort. This sensitivity serves to protect the vital reproductive organs.

rider follows and ropes him. The calf is thrown and tied. Later, if he's able to walk, he's led away; he may be bleeding or have broken bones. This poses no problem; of all rodeo animals, calves are the cheapest and thus the most expendable.

For the most part, rodeo animals are supplied by livestock contractors who specialize in the finding and conditioning of four-legged talent. Unbroken horses are preferred, for example, and they are encouraged to hate and distrust men so that they'll put on a good show. At home, at the rodeo, and on the road between rodeos, the animal stars are deliberately mistreated. The wild ones are mostly just nervous wrecks, but they are much in demand at rodeos, so their owners make a comfortable living.

Today's rodeo is a far cry from its beginnings. In the good old days, it was nothing more than an exhibition of working cowboy skills. The men demonstrated what they did every day back at the ranch and on the range. The cowboy was just coming into his own as an American hero, and the public was eager to see him roping a steer or curing a green horse of the bucks.

From that simple start, the rodeo evolved into the modern version, which is nothing more than show business on the most brutal level. It is sold as tradition or early Americana, but that is pure myth. What goes on at the ranch has no relation to what goes on at the rodeo. Only the placid steer packs on weight, and weight means profit, and that's what the ranch business is all about. The cowboy who busted a steer would find himself busted from employment. And the horses aren't provoked into bucking, they are broken to the saddle in easy stages, and few know abuse. Many a ranch owner has reason to curse the rodeo and does, for it has been the ruination of too many good cowpunchers. Back on the range, they just can't seem to forget the rodeo habits.

But the ranchers can't do anything about the rodeos, for control passed from their hands to the promoters a long time ago. It's not just show business these days, it's big business, and there must be times when the moneymakers feel that the world would be a wonderful place if it weren't for the humanitarians.

The rodeo world now has a governing body, though not all rodeos belong. Those that do take pride in the rules that prohibit cruelty to animals, though offending performers are merely docked a few points, not fined. So why don't the humane societies fade away? Because, while the intent of the rules is right, there is no supervision and very little enforcement. The Rodeo Cowboys Association doesn't believe in cruelty to animals, either. Its members don't mean to break backs or necks or legs, but "accidents" will happen. The cowboys are risking their necks to entertain the public, so why shouldn't the animals? "And don't forget that the rides are short," the rodeo riders remark, as if defining a cruelty as strictly a long-term thing.

Millions of innocent spectators find the rodeo a thrilling, exciting, entertaining event. But take away the cruelties that underlie the thrills and excitement and the rodeo world will fall on its face.

It's all in the hands of the states, but only Ohio is aware of that point. Just to make sure that its anticruelty laws would apply to the rodeo, Ohio's legislators plugged all possible loopholes by specifying, "No person shall directly or indirectly or by aiding, abetting, or permitting the doing thereof, put, place, fasten, use or fix upon or to any work animal used or readied for use for a work purpose, twisted wire snaffles, bucking straps, flank straps, electric or other prods or similar devices."

This came as quite a shock to the Rodeo Association, for its rules require the use of the bucking strap, and the bronco won't feel like bucking if it isn't binding into his flanks and penis, and especially if the electric prod isn't used. So while the rodeo is popular with Ohioans, the state is not popular with the rodeo promoters, and events are not on the increase there. Rodeo rules also require that a calf be thrown to the ground and a bull be twisted to the ground, two actions that might be regarded as cruelties to animals in Ohio, a very sensitive state.

Elsewhere, and that means almost every other state, the rodeo has managed to stay out of trouble while flaunting the existing anticruelty laws. The laws of the states are quite similar, and all agree that a person is guilty of cruelty if he pits one animal against another, or if he pits human against animal, or if he abuses, torments, goads, infuriates or incites an animal to react. The laws also stipulate that the owner, custodian or person present who encourages such actions is subject to prosecution.

In effect, the law's definition of cruelty applies to the events of the rodeo, but prosecution remains a seldom thing. The show appears to have the same built-in immunity as the medical laboratory, though it operates without federal grants. Its success in presenting animal abuse as entertainment has attracted a better class of cowboy, and some of today's top riders are college graduates who have never set foot on a ranch. The best collect from twenty to forty thousand a year in prize money, and they are as insensitive about animals now as they were in biology class not too many years ago.

Is it any wonder the Spanish don't understand us?

The Free Shows 5

THE SPECTATORS WHO PAY TO WATCH THE ABUSE OF RODEO animals are really spending their money needlessly. The livestock auction, a true American tradition, pride and joy of rural America, serves up an even greater variety of abuses, and admission is free.

The livestock auction, stock auction, farm commission auction—it has many names—serves an important need in the nation's farm economy. The auction is the place where farmers can find a ready market for odd lots of stock and poultry, and nobody knows how many such events take place each year. Some states have auction regulations, and some don't, so there are no exact records; but five thousand such auctions a year would be a conservative estimate, and to state that fifty million animals are involved yearly would be even more conservative.

The average auction is held in a big barn or out in the open, and in either place, there's more room for the people than the animals. A small space is reserved for the animals, and they are placed in that area when their time comes to go under the auctioneer's hammer.

It's a long day for the animals: cows, calves, horses, hogs, sheep, poultry—all of them surplus, or unproductive, or not worth keeping, and none of them prize specimens. Some may be cripples, and some diseased.

The day starts back on the farm, where the animals are loaded for the trip to the auction. For many, it's their first trip on wheels, so they are shoved, jabbed, dragged, beaten and prodded onto the truck. It's not unusual for cows, horses, sheep and hogs to make the trip together on an old truck with a limited amount of space, splintered boards and protruding bolts. Chances are that the cow who becomes a mother on the way will be trampled to death. The calf is sure of that fate.

Upon arrival at the auction site, the survivors stay right where they are on the truck until needed by the auctioneer. Or, if room is available, they may be unloaded and prodded into holding pens, where broken boards, protruding nails, glass, debris, manure and mud aggravate their misery. Some pens have water troughs, but they are seldom filled. Still, while the pen is just as crowded as the truck, the air is fresher.

A professional sadist would derive a great deal of enjoyment just from watching the trucks being unloaded. The auctioneer's assistants help the farmer in this chore, and the assistants are often muscular fellows who delight in exhibiting their strength. One will pick up a calf and toss it to the ground, a second will hold a lamb in each hand and then drop them, and a third may use a heavy iron rod to whack a stubborn horse over the head. In one way or another, the truck will be unloaded when the proper time comes, and no matter how rough the handling of the animals, there will always be onlookers who find the sight an occasion for laughter. Here too, the entertainment is free.

The auctioneer works as quickly as possible. It's his job to sell as many animals as possible—singly or in lots—at the highest possible prices, although those prices never soar. The seller knows his profit will be pennies per head, and he's anxious to realize what little he can. The bidders know that risks are involved, for farmers never auction off quality stock. Nobody makes much or loses much at an auction.

Hurried as the auction may be, most of the animals present—the sold and the waiting-to-be-sold—are there for many hours. The stock that is too obviously crippled will be shunted aside for a wait that sometimes extends into days before a meat processor arrives. If they are fed or watered during that time, the animals are lucky. All that matters is that the suffering animals be kept alive for the processor. Death begins the spoiling process in meat, so he won't buy corpses. Nor does he want severely bruised animals. There are laws to prevent the selling of bruised meat. So the bodies of those that die en route or at the auctions are dumped aside and hauled away at a later date.

All day long, trucks are arriving and departing with their cargoes of moaning, bawling, bleating animals. The cries of the animals, the shouts of the auctioneer, and the laughter of the milling people are the basic sound effects at any auction. And sometimes there is applause, as when a trembling, week-old calf is hauled to his feet and kicked into running, the better to prove that he's truly alive and worth fifty cents more than offered.

At most auctions, calves bring the most action.

Hundreds of thousands of them, hours old up to a few days old, change hands at the livestock auctions every year, and they are among the most abused animal babies in the world. Often separated from their mothers before they've had a chance to taste their first milk, the starving youngsters are trucked to the auction, driven into the holding pens and then into the sales ring, and there forced into activity. The driving and forcing is accomplished by strong men with a talent for twisting tails and ears, using electric prods, and wielding a board as if it were a club.

Coming and going, the frightened calves are pitiful sights. They may arrive in a truck crowded with other animals, or in the trunk of a passenger car, or in a box or a gunny sack. Many arrive with broken legs or obvious bruises. They are shunted aside and forgotten. Disposal comes later.

At the big auctions, it's not unusual for calves to be penned for several days before being purchased and transported to their new homes. Whether an individual calf lives or dies is of no real concern to the buyer. The price is cheap, the buyer is playing the numbers game, and if enough live his gamble will pay off. At a dollar or two a head, the buyer figures that he can't lose.

Calves, like all young animals, are delicate live things, susceptible to extremes of heat and cold, as well as to a great number of diseases. But the digestive process of the calf makes him even more delicate than most other animals, and only natural feeding, or artificial feeding closely resembling the natural, will bring him through the first few days in good health.

Except for the idiots among them, all farmers know that a cow's milk is unfit for human consumption for a period of five days following calving. For five days then, the calf is not an expense to the legitimate dairy farmer, nor is he a real expense for the next month, when skim milk and calf meal would suffice to keep him in good health and give him a sound start in life. But the quick dollar is more important to most farmers, and there are probably angry men in a few states where the law prohibits the sale of any calf under the age of four weeks. Oddly, those laws were made to protect human health (from diseases which a very young animal may harbor unnoticed), and not with the calf's welfare in mind.

The majority of the calves offered at auctions are the males. They have no future on the average farm but are always in demand as potential veal. So the auction calf, if he lives to see his new home, has a life expectancy of six to eight more weeks. They can be very unpleasant weeks, especially if the new owner has his mind set on producing white veal, a color that does not mean superior taste or tenderness, although the consumer public may believe so. The veal raisers intent on satisfying the public have all sorts of theories, none of them pleasant for the calves. Thus, gourmets who prefer their veal white may owe thanks to a calf who (1) was raised in total darkness (Theory: sunlight colors flesh), or (2) was bled from time to time (Theory: blood colors flesh), or (3) was fed only liquids (Theory: roughage colors flesh), or (4) was kept in close confinement and with no bedding (roughage) (Theory: close confinement increases rate of growth, which in turn increases white flesh).

The men who sell and buy at auctions, and the men who practice the white veal theories are regarded with disdain by those other lovers of livestock, the cattlemen. The men who raise the beef know all about the auctions and they know that the calves are treated miserably. What sort of man would rip a day-old calf from his mother's side?

The rancher treats calves differently. He needs them, for he would go out of business without them, and as far as he can help it, no calf of his will ever be mistreated. Of course, when a man is running ten or twenty thousand head of cattle, he can't be expected to supervise all of them all of the time. So in the cold of winter or the heat of summer, cows are on their own when calving time arrives, and it's touch and go for the newborn. It's a matter of the survival of the fittest, and the calves who live and grow may look back to blizzards as friendly things compared to man—for their first contact with man is anything but a pleasant experience.

The young bull's first contact starts with a rope around his neck and a rude jerk that spills him to the ground. His hind legs are quickly bound, and then he's dragged off to the fire area. There, held firmly to the ground by the cowboys, he can do no more than bawl his agony as the red-hot branding iron burns into his rump flesh. The pain is intense, and the men do nothing to relieve it. In fact, he is subjected to even greater pain as an expert seizes the testes and slices away with the blade of a huge knife. This is castration of the crudest sort, completed without anesthetic or medication, although a disinfectant is sometimes slopped over the bloody wound.

The series of pains isn't over yet. A long hypodermic needle pierces the young bull's hide, and a serum is injected to provide immunity against certain diseases. He's nearly unconscious from pain and shock now, and he can do no more than moan as a knife blade sinks and twists into his head, and then again. His starting horns have been removed, and now a caustic solution is rubbed into the open wounds to kill further horn growth.

At no time, on the day of all the misery or during the painful days that follow, does the calf receive any relief from man. It is assumed that the calf will recover, and he probably will. If he survives and reaches maturity, he'll meet the friendly men again.

This time they'll herd him and others to the proper assembly point, and there all will be beaten, jabbed and prodded until they realize they are supposed to climb into the truck or boxcar. Whatever the means of transportation, overcrowding and scarcity or actual lack of food and water are the rule. For the cattle—and the story is the same for sheep and hogs—the ride to the livestock market becomes another fight for survival. Many are maimed and battered by the time they reach the marketplace, and some are dead.

Millions of pounds of meat are wasted in this manner every year. The lack of supervision and the carelessness of owners is difficult to understand—after all, livestock is their bread and butter—unless one is aware of the magic known as insurance. By insuring his load, the owner (shipper) is paid by the insurance carrier for all animals dead upon arrival at the marketplace. So the owner can't lose, and he couldn't care less about the welfare of his stock.

In one recent year, incomplete livestock exchange figures revealed these "dead on arrival" totals: more than 38,000 hogs, 25,000 sheep, and 14,000 steers. "Alive but bruised" tallies were several times higher. Bruised meat is not supposed to be sold for human consumption; it should be trimmed out and if so, represents sheer waste to the packers. The dead and the bruised help explain the high cost of meat at the consumer level.

The needless waste has not gone unnoticed by American business. Shippers and handlers of livestock have been undergoing an educational program launched by Livestock Conservation, Inc., a group of packers, livestock exchange officials, railroad men and truckers. The conservation is profit-inspired, of course, but it has already achieved results and, indirectly, made "the last ride" a less cruel experience for hundreds of thousands of animals. The railroads and the big truckers have done the most to improve shipping conditions. But in many areas things are pretty much the same as they were fifty years ago. The small ranchers don't care, the small truckers don't care, and the insurance companies don't mind too much. Why coddle the meat animals? Haven't percentages always paid off in the past?

So today—right now—all over the country, trucks are rolling up to the unloading docks at livestock markets with their mixed cargoes of the living, the dead, the crippled and the bruised. For many hours or several days, they are exposed to the most adverse conditions: lack of ventilation, food and water; overcrowding, heat and humidity. Many ranchers and truckers do not understand this. They realize that humans could not withstand such conditions, but they feel that livestock should. And they regard the big truckers with suspicion. Where's the profit in treating dumb animals to new equipment, air conditioning, rest periods and checking stations?

From the unloading docks at the reception centers, the still-walking swine, cattle and sheep are herded into holding pens. The reluctant ones are encouraged to move a bit faster by the application of the good old electric prod. For those who underestimate the potency of the prod: tests done on dressed meat two hours after the host animals were slaughtered revealed first-degree burns inflicted by it. Does any rodeo lover still wonder why a bull bounces or a bronco jumps for the sky or a calf runs a hundred yards in world-record time?

So, thanks to the prod, the animals are herded quickly into the holding pens. There, at least, they enjoy fresh air and room to move. If the time schedule permits, they may even find water or food or both. It's as if man, at the next to the last moment, feels guilty and wants to demonstrate that he's capable of a little kindness.

The animal doesn't know it, but his next steps will be in the direction of the slaughterhouse. If he lags, the electric prod will be there to hurry him to his doom.

He is on the threshold of another chamber of horrors.

The Slaughterhouse 6

NO OTHER AMERICAN INSTITUTION IS SO APTLY NAMED. And if every one of our slaughterhouses were constructed of glass, this would be a nation of vegetarians.

Who among us would savor a roast of pork after witnessing this scene:

A hog is driven into a pen, shackled around one hind leg, then hoisted aloft by a mechanical pulley. He dangles there, head down, within convenient reach of the man assigned to slash his throat. The man approaches and curses, for the hog is uncooperative. The big animal is frightened and in pain. He squeals and thrashes and may have already fractured his shackled leg or his pelvis, thus adding to his agony. The impatient man drops his knife, picks up a sledgehammer (or poleax) and swings for a point between the hog's eyes. His aim is faulty and he hits an eye. A second swing hits the nose. Finally the battered hog's wild antics cease. The man goes back to the knife and slashes the hog's throat, then steps back, releases the hoist rope, and plunges the animal into a vat of scalding water. Bleeding from the throat, one eye knocked out, his nose smashed, but still living and conscious, the hog disappears in the scalding water and dies there.

That's the way it was for pigs, sheep and cattle in most of our slaughterhouses before 1958, the year of the Humane Slaughter Law, a federal law. And law or no law, that's the way it is today in many, many American slaughterhouses. Tens of millions of animals—steers, calves, sheep, lambs—are slaughtered annually in this barbaric way. When it comes to cruelties, those connected with the production and marketing of food animals far exceed those encountered in all other phases of animal usage by man.

Around a billion and a half quadruped food animals are slaughtered for our tables every year. Less than twenty percent are slaughtered by relatively humane methods. Still, thanks to the years spent by individuals and groups trying to better slaughterhouse conditions, this is progress of a sort. Not much, but better than nothing.

The crusade started as far back as 1865, when Henry Bergh, founder of the American humane movement, denounced the slaughtering methods of the day, methods that are still with us today. Year after year, the crusade achieved absolutely nothing in the way of results. Then, in 1929, there was a little ray of sunshine: the mighty meat packing industry itself announced that it was going to do something about reforms. But nothing happened.

It was not until 1954 that definite steps were taken to end the atrocities of the slaughterhouse. Credit Congressman William Dawson of Utah with introducing a bill to eliminate the major cruelties: "That their collective screams of pain (swine, sheep, lambs) are heard only by a few, does not lessen the general guilt once we have been made aware of the practice. What we will not condone in one cruelty against one defenseless animal, we cannot condone in an industry—however valuable and necessary—against a mass of defenseless animals."

Dawson's bill served to expose the atrocities as they had never been exposed before, and the general public found the charges hard to believe. But if the layman was shocked, his reaction was as nothing compared to the meatman's anger. The various factions of the meat industry, led by the packers, marched to Washington and insisted that existing methods were best, and that any other methods would be too expensive. This wasn't the only argument pressed by the meat industry, but it was the strongest, for it carried the implication that reforms would cause higher meat prices. And what elected official in his right mind would vote for higher prices?

For over ninety years, the meat industry had to know that a day of reckoning was coming, but in all that time it had not, apparently, looked around to find more humane and more economical ways to slaughter food animals. So finally, in 1954, humanitarians and humane organizations, at their own expense, took a look around. They found that there were humane methods available which were both economical and efficient, and they had been used successfully for years in Europe, where the law requires that animals be rendered insensible to pain before they are slaughtered. Among these practical, humane methods were:

1) Carbon dioxide gas—can be used on sheep, calves and swine; animals to whom it is administered "pass out" quickly and calmly.

2) Electric stunning—can be used on sheep, calves, swine, goats and cattle; electric current is administered so as to produce surgical anesthesia instantly.

3) Mechanical devices—can be used on sheep, calves, swine, goats, cattle, horses and mules; such as capture bolt stunners and firearms.

Slaughtering animals in a humane fashion was thus not a problem, but our own meat industry had taken no obvious steps to find that out for itself. The need for legislation was apparent to all. New voices were heard, and they included the eleven million members of the General Federation of Women's Clubs: "Cruelty to animals in our slaughterhouses has been thus far permitted only because, it is argued, brutality is cheaper than decency. The immorality of the argument is obvious." And from the newly formed National Humane Society (now the Humane Society of the United States): "In the best slaughterhouses in America, with two or three exceptions, the methods of killing animals are cruel. In many, the brutality is unspeakable. There has been no national organization that has been willing and able to fight national cruelties."

The late Senator Richard C. Neuberger of Oregon and the then Senator Hubert H. Humphrey of Minnesota cosponsored a humane slaughter bill in the Senate.

From Neuberger:

> Barbaric cruelty is wrong in a moral nation. I would cosponsor the bill that we are introducing even if enactment would cause some monetary loss to packers, livestock producers and consumers of meat. There can be no price tag on cruelty. Suffering should not be a part of profits. . . . There are humane methods already available and developed to a point of efficiency which can actually achieve savings, rather than added costs, for farmers, industry, and for housewives doing the family food shopping.

From Humphrey:

> It is time that we in the United States faced the fact that we trail behind much of the world in adoption of approved and humane practices in slaughter of animals for food. What we are asking in the legislation is already accepted and in use in many other countries. We pride ourselves in being advanced in technology in most of our endeavors; we should be just as advanced in humane regard for handling and treatment of animals.

Finally, Congress passed the Neuberger-Humphrey bill: The Humane Slaughter Law, 1958. It took a long time: from Bergh in 1865 to Dawson, Neuberger and Humphrey in 1958, a period covering 93 years and too many billions of brutally slaughtered animals.

The bill was hailed as one of the greatest victories ever won for animals. President Eisenhower signed it into law, and Senator Humphrey summed up the long, legislative battle with the words, "I believe that we witnessed, during the campaign for slaughterhouse reform, one of those spontaneous manifestations of basic goodness and decency with which the American people every once in a while indicate that they may be worthy to lead a troubled world in progress toward peace and justice."

The Humane Slaughter Law outlawed the poleax, the shackle and the hoist. It called for such humane methods as instantaneous stunning and anesthetization before the moment of actual slaughter. It placed Washington itself above reproach: "No government agency may buy meat or meat products from any packer who in any of his plants, or a plant of any subsidiary company, slaughters animals inhumanely or handles animals inhumanely in connection with slaughter." At the time, the Government was buying around 300 million dollars worth of meat a year, and it was felt that the provision would exert strong economic coercion on the packers.

It did—on some of the big packers. They were the only ones selling to the Government anyway. The thousands of small slaughterhouses never have and never will, so they are under no pressure. The majority of them still operate as of old, for the law was designed not to offend states' rights, and it had to be supplemented by state laws. To date, only nineteen of our states have backed the federal law. So the great victory was not an overwhelming one, and the federal buying provision, while well meant, was not a match for American business ingenuity. As long as his meat source is not a subsidiary, a packer selling to the Government and running short on beef, for example, can buy from a slaughterhouse that still uses the inhumane methods. Meanwhile (since 1958) the Government buying of meat has zoomed.

But back in 1958, the Act appeared to be a stunning defeat for the meat industry. A mood of complacency drifted over most humanitarians, and one famous, national organization voted its Seal of Approval to a leading packer who purchased the humane, instantaneous stunners for use on cattle. The packer was happy to accept the seal, and forgot to mention that he was still using the poleax, shackle and hoist on swine and sheep. It was just a minor deception, especially compared to one contained in the law itself.

This was in the form of a couple of amendments that were designed to appease the proponents of Jewish ritual slaughter. This ritual slaughter, or *schechita*, employs the shackle and hoist, and calls for the animal to be conscious at the moment of slaughter. Thus, the federal law that found the shackling and hoisting of conscious animals to be illegal and inhumane found the same process to be legal and humane where ritual slaughter was concerned. This may not have been the greatest contradiction to come out of Washington, but it remains one of the best.

In all of our states then, including the nineteen which have outlawed the shackle and hoist, the kosher slaughterhouses have immunity from the law. This immunity has not gone unnoticed, of course, and the controversy over *schechita* has been intense for almost a decade. Today, things stand pretty much as they did back in 1961 when The Humane Society of the United States prepared an analysis of the situation. The HSUS reported, in part:

> In mid-1958 the Congress of the United States enacted, and the President signed, a national law declaring it to be the policy of the United States that livestock be slaughtered humanely. The Act defines humane slaughter and requires Federal agencies to buy meat only from packers that conform to the national policy.
>
> The Jewish ritual method of slaughter is defined by the Federal law as humane. The language of that section of the Federal law was drafted by a committee officially representing a group of Jewish organizations, including such diverse organizations as the Union of Orthodox Rabbis and the American Jewish Congress.
>
> Humane slaughter laws are officially sponsored and endorsed by some more than 600 American humane societies, by the General Federation of Women's Clubs, the Methodist Church, the Southern Baptist Convention, the National Catholic Society for Animal Welfare, many other religious groups, the Amalgamated Meat Cutters and Butcher Workmen of North America, AFL-CIO, and by hundreds of other organizations, and most of the American press.
>
> Packers also support this legislation. At legislative hearings in California, the President of the Western States Meat Packers Association twice testified in favor of a humane slaughter bill that has been enacted. In Wisconsin, top executives of Armour, Cudahy, and Jones Farm Sausage Company testified in support of similar legislation. In Tennessee, every packer in the

state informed the legislature that it had no objection to enactment of such legislation.

Opposition to humane slaughter legislation currently comes virtually exclusively from a group of organizations that purports to speak for all American Jews. Real opposition to humane slaughter laws comes almost exclusively from ultra-orthodox rabbis, particularly members of the Union of Orthodox Rabbis, but they have achieved the official, nominal support of the following organizations: American Jewish Congress, Central Conference of American Rabbis, Jewish Labor Committee, Jewish War Veterans of the United States, Rabbinical Assembly of America, Rabbinical Council of America, Synagogue Council of America, Union of American Hebrew Congregations, Union of Orthodox Jewish Congregations of America, United Synagogues of America, also state, county and local Jewish community councils affiliated with the National Community Relations Advisory Council.

In appearances before committees of many state legislatures and in public print, the Jewish opponents of humane slaughter legislation have rested exclusively on two assertions: (1) This legislation would outlaw *schechita;* and (2) This legislation would make ritual slaughter economically impractical or impossible.

No other argument against the proposed legislation has been seriously advanced by any responsible spokesman for the opponents.

Over the past few years, New York City and its environs have emerged as the nation's hotbed of activity in the fight for humane slaughter. Students of the subject may find this rather odd, for New York State has never supplemented the federal law and most of the meat (except for pork, of course) and fowl consumed in the big-city area comes from the busy, nearby kosher slaughter-houses. Ritual slaughter enjoys—if that's the word—double immunity, and just about every New Yorker (those against inhumane slaughter, those for *schechita*, and those who don't care) dines on meat that went through shackling and hoisting on the way to the table.

Sensitivity is the order of the day. When Friends of Animals, Inc., a humane group, stated in a *New York Times* advertisement that it objected to the "brutally cruel practice" of shackling and hoisting conscious animals prior to slaughter, the Long Island Commission of Rabbis, Inc., filed a one-million-dollar libel suit against the group, the *Times*, and 58 private individuals. The rabbis felt that kosher slaughter had been "maliciously ascribed as being motivated by economic issues rather than religious beliefs." And on a recent WOR radio panel, rabbis accused critics of ritual slaughter of being anti-Semitic.

Humanitarians, of course, come in both sexes, all ages, and all religions. Their objections to ritual slaughter do not make them anti-Semitics. If they do, then the designation applies to the Jewish humanitarians who object to ritual slaughter, too.

Both those who defend old-fashioned slaughter methods, as in *schechita*, and those who find those methods abhorrent have been unable to convince each other. The politicians, unable to get an accurate nose-count, keep as far as possible from the debate. And the general public is more concerned with meat quality than meat preparation. Or can it be that the public still hasn't grasped the difference between one type of slaughter and another? If that's the case, here's an HSUS word picture:

> Actually, the existing Federal law and similar state laws are not really aimed at the method of slaughtering livestock. These laws are aimed, rather, at controlling the method of handling and holding animals in preparation for the act of slaughter. In American packing plants, 99 percent of all animals slaughtered are killed by severing the blood vessels of the throat with a knife, whether or not the killing is conducted according to any ritual. Except in the case of swine, the slaughter of which is not an issue here, the ritual and non-ritual methods of slaughtering animals in American packing plants are physically almost identical.
>
> The essential difference between the ritual killing of animals and other slaughtering results from the ritual requirement that animals come to the slaughter uninjured (at least in any major organ). That requirement means, according to modern American rabbinical interpretation, that animals must be fully conscious at the moment that the "schechita" uses his knife. In non-ritual slaughter, it is permissible for animals to be previously anesthetized or humanely stunned by mechanical equipment or electricity.
>
> It must further be understood that the almost universal method in American packing plants of delivering animals to the man who uses the knife, whether he be a "schechita" following the Jewish ritual or only an ordinary packing plant employee, is to shackle a chain around one hind leg of the animal

and then hoist the animal from the floor, head down, with power machinery.

There is ample testimony in the records of Congress to prove that this procedure dislocates leg joints, tears tendons and muscles, ruptures blood vessels, and causes great agony to the animals. Animals frequently hang in that position for five or ten minutes before being killed. It is this brutal treatment of animals prior to the moment of slaughter that we are trying to outlaw. Such cruelty is, of course, no part of the ritual of any religion. It is a cruelty invented by packers, certainly unknown to Moses or to the pages of the Talmud.

This cruelty has been outlawed, when slaughter is not by ritual, by the Federal humane slaughter act and all similar state laws. The Federal law and the state laws require that animals killed non-ritually shall be anesthetized or humanely otherwise made unconscious before they are shackled, hoisted, or cut.

It should be carefully noted that no bill ever proposed to Congress or any legislature has proposed that animals going to ritual slaughter should be anesthetized or otherwise stunned before slaughter. It has been proposed only that packers be required to bring animals into position for ritual slaughter with devices and methods that do not cause injury or pain. It is this proposed requirement that is being so fiercely opposed by the orthodox rabbinate and, apparently, by almost the entire American Jewish Community.

The proposal that animals be handled without injury or pain prior to ritual slaughter is entirely practical, both mechanically and economically. Great Britain and most European nations have had laws embodying such a requirement for many years. In no case, in any nation, has such a law proved to be oppressive or

> even to create a difficulty. The orthodox rabbinate of Canada has stated publicly that methods of handling animals now being used in Canadian packing plants are fully satisfactory.
>
> The United States Department of Agriculture, Bureau of Meat Inspection, has said that it will require a few minor modifications of Canadian methods if they are adopted in the United States, solely in the interest of a strict sanitary code, but the Department of Agriculture has also officially said that it sees no difficulty in the way of achieving the recommended modifications. The Department of Agriculture officially accepts, without changes, humane casting pens [which confine animal in a position for slaughter] that long have been in use in Great Britain and elsewhere in Europe.

In a nutshell then, the barbaric shackle and the cruel hoist have long since been outlawed in Canada, Great Britain, and many European countries. In those enlightened countries, no exception is made for ritual slaughter.

Nonetheless, ritual slaughter continues in those countries. *Schechita* is still performed, but without the preliminary shackle and hoist. The rabbis remain orthodox, the meat is accepted as kosher, and the world hasn't come to an end.

Is kosher meat less kosher overseas?

Do the needless cruelties inflicted upon the animals make kosher meat more kosher in this country?

Does an American Orthodox Jew eat meat when he travels abroad?

What does he do when in Switzerland, where ritual slaughter has been banned altogether?

While we ponder these questions, more millions of animals are being shackled and hoisted. Not all over the world, of course. Mostly in the United States.

The Blood Lovers 7

UNLESS HE'S ASSOCIATED WITH THE MEAT INDUSTRY, the average citizen seldom visits the slaughterhouse. If he does, he never visits again. A little strong, and hardly the place to take the wife and family, or friends from out of town. Even the blood lovers, those medievalists of the sporting set, avoid the slaughterhouse, for the action is too one-sided and everybody knows the animal can't win. It's strictly no contest.

The blood lovers prefer a contest in which each side, or each contestant, has an equal chance. For this reason, they consider bullfighting inhumane and would prefer to watch a bull fighting a bull. They see nothing wrong in pitting animal against animal. What's inhumane about that, since no human is directly involved in the violence, and animals will fight one another anyway?

There are millions of these enthusiasts in America, and because of them two major, unpublicized "sports" continue to thrive: cockfighting and dogfighting. For economic reasons, there are more cockfights than dogfights. More than 8,000 cockfights in 1967, for example, despite the fact that they are illegal in every state except Florida. Specific laws, anticruelty laws, or gambling laws make such fights illegal in all the other states. All of the states, including Florida, have outlawed dogfighting. The blood lovers who prefer dogs to cocks think that

Florida is discriminating and that the Supreme Court should do something about it.

Cockfighting is now a multimillion-dollar business and the action takes place in every state, from coast to coast. The sport has its "game clubs," but membership rosters are as secret as those of the Ku Klux Klan. Whereas kennel clubs have the American Kennel Club and cat clubs have the Cat Fanciers Association, the game clubs have no national organization or governing body. Apparently, a central authority would be a hindrance, for the sport's popularity increases from year to year as more game clubs are formed for the purpose of staging fights.

If any one fact is responsible for holding the clubs together in their common cause, it is the fact that at least four national magazines are exclusively devoted to cockfighting. These special-interest publications all carry general news of the sport, list scheduled fights and dates, and advertise such items of interest to blood lovers as cocks, breeding stock, patent medicines, conditioners and gaffs. Gross sales of advertisers run to about ten million dollars a year.

The magazines and the sport itself are grateful to the Federal Government, for it would be difficult to get fresh news into the hands of subscribers if it weren't for the second-class mailing privileges. Second-class mail is, of course, a losing proposition for the Government, but Congress voted the low rate to encourage the dissemination of educational and cultural materials. So Florida doesn't stand alone. The Government apparently agrees that cockfighting is cultural, and every taxpayer in the land is helping to subsidize the sport.

Most of the time, this cultural sport takes place at night, and a big barn on an isolated farm is the common setting. Anywhere from a hundred to five hundred spectators attend the average cockfight, which is really a series of five. Weather, the reputations of the feathered contestants, and the conflict of fight dates determine attendance—but distance is never a factor. Half of the audience at any fight is usually from out of state, so eager are the fanciers of the sport.

They sit on wooden planks arranged in tiers so that all present may have a clear view of the action in the "cockpit." This is a circle of hard-packed earth, some fifteen feet in diameter, and it is ringed by a short sidewall plus fencing and a rail. Each fighting cock has a handler, known in the sport as a "cocker," and entrances for each gentleman and his bird are provided on opposite sides of the pit.

So the setting is simple, although it is sometimes difficult to see what transpires in the pit. Cigar and cigarette smoke hang heavy. The birds fight, the blood lovers watch, and all are enclosed in a firetrap. The sport disregards fire laws as it does all other laws.

Happy shouts of approval fill the old barn when the cockers enter the pit with their feathered charges. The cocks are no longer handsome birds, for their wings have been pruned, rumps and hackles shortened, and combs cut as close to the head as possible. This minimizes the target areas, and is also the reason why the breeding of fighting cocks has been declining in California. In that state, the law forbids comb cutting. It's a painful operation for the cock, of course, and the owner of a combless cock has some explaining to do. "In a certain district in California at one time were some of the largest breeders in the state," one of the lovers of the sport wrote in the magazine *Grit and Steel*. "They carried ads in *Grit and Steel*, some full pages, but today you rarely see a small one. California has some, but you won't see it in print because that is all the humane society wants. Just have one trimmed cock and if you own the property they will take that, too, before they are through with you."

But back to the pit, where the cockers are tying gaffs over the normal spurs of their birds. A gaff is a steel stiletto, three inches long, curved, and needle-sharp. Now the cocks are ready for business, and the cockers work them into a fury by warming them up—thrusting them not quite within reach of each other. Finally, at the order of "Pit 'em" from the judge, the birds are released and rush into battle. The two warriors slash, spur, jab, dodge, fly and jump, each intent on killing the other. If they go down with gaffs entangled, they are separated and released again. Between rounds, the handler may stick his bird's head into his own mouth, to warm the bird's damaged brain. Or he may blow on his bird's wounds, to prevent stiffening and to stop the flow of blood. Then it's back to the war again.

The fight continues until one bird can no longer fight. That means he's dead or near dead. In any event, his fighting career is over. Half the fights end that way, with one bird dead or soon destroyed. In most of the other fights, both cocks—the winner as well as the loser—are damaged beyond repair, and often both birds die in the pit.

As long as the obvious loser, whatever his condition, continues to fight, the judge permits the combat. The spectators don't like a loser, of course, but they recognize courage when they see it, so they shout encouragement to the maimed and dying bird. It's a rare fight when eyes aren't gouged out, or abdomens slit, or wings and legs broken, to mention a few of the results. As one of the sport's magazines put it: "In a protracted battle of two hours, it happens very often that a cock loses the beak, one or both eyes, and sometimes the skull is laid open, to say nothing of the injuries the bird receives in wings and body. But after each pause, they fall in with a will and seldom yield. Of course, now and then one of the cocks squawks or flies the pit to the embarrassment of his backers and the natural consternation of his breeders. To be spared this humiliation, the fanciers go to no end of trouble."

The sport's suppliers try to spare the fanciers such humiliation by offering big, proven fighting cocks ($100), worm medicine ($2), superior gaffs ($20), such conditioning medicines as the one ($5) that supposedly stops a cut cock from hemorrhaging, and razor-sharp knives ($15) designed to be fitted onto the cock's breast. These items, and more, can be bought through the mail any day of the week.

The men who breed fighting cocks—as either a vocation or avocation—are as intense about this activity as the store clerk-philatelist who put ten children through college. They are outstanding students of genetics and thus careful blenders of such ancient, brave bloodlines as Dominiques, Irish Grays, Eslin Red-Quills and the many Piles. Those lines trace back through the centuries, and are themselves mixes of other fighting lines that are presumed to go back more than three thousand years. So if the bloodlines are right, and the breeders make sure of that, then the cocks are hatched to fight, which is why they would rather fight than eat.

They do eat, of course, and they are probably the only fowl on earth to be fed raw meat. It whets their taste for blood, so to speak. No other fowl is massaged, either. Alcohol and ammonia, or other special lotions, are used to toughen their skins. After a short training period—just a couple of mock fights with padded spurs—the cocks are ready for the real thing. Usually they are a year old, although one with real promise may be held off for another six months or so.

Some of our finest citizens are breeders: scientists, professors, bankers, elected officials, justices of the peace, and of course, biology teachers. Together, they might be able to solve some of the world's problems. As it is, they work independently and add to the world's cruelties. Ask any one of them why he raises game birds and he'll reply that he's a trout fisherman and uses their feathers to tie his own flies. If he's a Floridian, of course, he doesn't need an excuse. And all of them dream of being the judge at a truly important cockfight. The assignment is an honor comparable to the winning of the Nobel prize.

Nobody knows how many people earn their living, in whole or part, from the sport of cockfighting, but their ranks include editors, suppliers, breeders, handlers, gamblers, fight promoters, and owners of old, rentable barns. In this land of the free, they feel they have a perfect right to earn a living in any way they see fit—so long as they are not hurting "anybody," and a cock is certainly nobody. They are moralists, too, and claim that their sport is much more fair than that other sport, hunting: fighting cocks are matched within two ounces of each other, but what chance does a feeble little rabbit have against a 12-gauge shotgun and a man? And many of them argue that cockfighting is no less than God's own will: throw feed on the ground, then throw two starving cocks on the ground, and the cocks will fight instead of eat. Thus cocks were created for the purpose of fighting. And what about the famous Americans who enjoyed cockfighting in times past? George Washington, for instance.

This reasoning is encouraged by the magazines, of course, although not in all issues. Some editorial space must be devoted to advice: "I maintain that no cockfight can be held without knowledge of the local law enforcement lads, and that friendly relations for such meets should be established before any attempt is made to hold them."

Not new advice, but very sound and worth repeating at least once a year as the new game clubs join the ranks.

Anyone engaged in humane society work would agree also that it is proven advice, for when society agents and cooperating local law officers stage their midnight raids, the raids are rarely successful. The barn is there and the pit is there, and sometimes people who haven't heard the news are there, but for some reason the fighting cocks are missing. Either the law has been too cooperative—with everybody—or the fight promoters have read the latest issues of their favorite magazine:

> It is a good plan to have a gatekeeper in a position at least a hundred yards from the pit building. A rope across the road will do, and let him stop all cars there, with the actual ticket selling done at the pit building. He should be in contact with the pit by individual direct phone or by "walkie-talkie," so in the event of a visit by the Law he is able to let the boys in the pit know in advance of the visit.

Fortunately, not all of the fighting-cock fanciers pay attention to such advice, and not all local law officers are cooperative in the extreme. So a small percentage of the raids have been and continue to be successful, but fines are small and meaningless, just an accepted part of the game to the devoted fancier. A cockfighting arrest doesn't lower his stature in the community. Indeed, when word gets around, strangers and friends may approach him with requests for tickets to the next fight.

Generally, though, law enforcement amounts to no more than a big joke. In every state, certain counties are famous as hosts to cockfights, and their reputations grow year after year. It's common knowledge, so common that only the local police haven't heard about it. When two hundred cars with blazing headlights turn into the same gravel road, the passengers aren't going to a Mafia meeting. And none of the cars are speeding. So why should the police investigate?

Two hundred cars heading down a dirt road on a Sunday morning constitute another sight that rural police do not find unusual. They assume that the people are going to church. One must be something of an historian to appreciate the humor of their assumption: right from the beginning, New England frowned upon cockfighting, so the cockfighting enthusiasts staged their matches when the good people were in church. Traditionalists among the blood lovers still prefer the morning of the Sabbath to the late-at-night events.

Massachusetts was the first state to outlaw the cockfight. It happened in 1836, or too long ago for the cockfight enthusiasts to remember. That state and New York share the dubious honor of playing host to the most cockfights per annum in the East.

Oddly, the devotees of cockfights seldom graduate to the dogfights. It may be because chicken is a favorite dinner dish in America, and the dog is not. Our minds may be warped, but our tastes remain Occidental. Or perhaps a social distinction separates the blood lovers: if any of our best citizens belong to the dogfight fancy, police records don't prove it.

Dogfighting, illegal in every state under one law or another, has been defined in one of the sport's own magazines as "the cruelest game since Rome." It may be. Certainly it is a brutal sport, far bloodier than cockfighting and more difficult to find if one is not an active fancier or a subscriber to the sport's magazines. While scheduled fights are held every week in every state, there's just no way of knowing or even estimating the total number of combats. Private fights arranged between owners, both of them heavy gamblers, are more numerous than those announced and held before an audience. Often, the private fight is a case of necessity, as when the owner of a successful, feared dog must travel a thousand miles to find a worthy challenger. But when the stakes are right, distance means nothing.

At the present, there are approximately 25,000 dogs fighting for a living in the United States, or, more precisely, fighting to make a living for their owners, of which there are about three thousand. While these totals are not impressive compared to those of cockfighting, the dog sport has been around a long time and has enjoyed a steady if not phenomenal growth. It is also looking to the future. In a recent magazine article, one of the sport's elders suggested that more teen-age boys be invited to witness fights so that they might realize "the many hours of real enjoyment" they've been missing. If the elder has his way, the nation's juvenile delinquent population will be aided in its increase.

According to the sport's historians, today's fighting dog traces his ancestry back to the Merry England of two centuries ago, when bull-baiting contests were even more popular than cockfights. The dogs who tormented the bulls were a cross between the Bulldog and the Rat Terrier. This cross was enhanced by the bloods of other breeds, and the fighting dog was born. He was used first in man-dog fights, and finally—thanks to a shortage of human opponents—to fight other dogs. Now England had both fighting dogs and dogfights, and the new sport spread like wildfire. It was declared illegal in 1835, and ever since the dogfights in England have been private affairs and not popular. Today a planned dogfight is a rare happening in the British Isles.

When the sport was revived, the revival came in this country, and it was limited to local matches. Then, as the various states fell into line with their anti-cruelty-to-animals laws, dogfighting spread out and became an interstate activity. If there is such a thing as an underground sport, this is it. There are just too many dog lovers around, and—from a blood lover's point of view—the less said and written about dogfights, the better off the sport will be.

The fighting dog which is popular in the United States should not be confused with the modern Bull Terrier, although some of that breed's blood is in him. The fighter is lean, round-headed and shorteared. He comes in solid and multiple colors, usually white or brindle or fawn. Fighting weight is about forty pounds, and the dog may lose several pounds during a battle. He can also lose his life.

He is a product of many, many generations of selective breeding. The same may be said for all the pure breeds of dogs, of course, but most have been bred with overall improvement in mind. The fighter has been bred to improve his viciousness, and pups in a litter must be separated soon after weaning. Fighting pups play for keeps.

The young dogs are kept in separate pens, or they may be staked out at a safe distance from one another. If litter brother does not strain to get at litter brother, he's a poor prospect for the pit and may, at a later date, be used as training bait for his brother.

A fighting dog is trained, or "worked" all during his growing period. A common starting method calls for harnessing the dog and then attaching the harness to the end of a long, revolving pole. The dog moves only in a circle, and he does so in attempting to reach a basket that contains a cat, chicken, rabbit or some other form of animal life. When he has worked himself into a fury of frustration, he is permitted to reach the basket and tear its occupant to shreds. During the advanced stages of his training, he is tossed into a room that holds several stolen pets: cats, dogs, or both. This sharpens his killing instinct.

Now, after long months of preparation, the novice is ready for his first fight. He represents quite an investment, in money as well as time. The stud fee for a top dog among legitimate pet breeders will seldom run to more than five hundred dollars. In the fighting fancy, a stud fee of several thousand dollars is not unusual.

The dog's owner brings him along slowly by trying to outwit other owners by matching his newcomer with lesser opponents. It doesn't take long to judge a dog's fighting ability. If he wins his first fight, and if his owner is smart enough to let him recuperate for several months before his second fight, and then he wins that one, the dog is on his way to a career. His career can end in any future fight, for now he has a reputation and his opponents will be veterans in the game. A few victories over the veterans and the fighter is ready for the big time, as the "conventions" are known.

A convention is the top event in the dogfighting world, and there's nothing annual about it. There can be several conventions a week, each taking place in several parts of the country, and each scheduled far in advance. The convention host is always a man of integrity, a man the fancy trusts. He sets the date and site and attends to all preparations, including immunity from the law. Maryland, Georgia, both Carolinas, Texas, Missouri, Ohio and Mississippi are popular convention states, and they attract dogs from all over the country. The owner lists his best dogs and the money he's willing to wager on each, and there are always takers. Each fight thus arranged is known as an invitation match.

The conventions are well attended and well protected. In the last few years, there has been no recorded instance of a successful raid. It's not that humane society agents aren't aware of conventions, but they've found it impossible to convince rural law officers that dogfights can happen.

But they do. The setting, unless it's a private fight, is similar to that of a cockfight. A barn in some remote area, a pit, and benches for spectators. Audiences are naturally larger at the conventions, for this is where the nearest thing to a championship can be won, and the dogs are ready and rested for the fray. Owners of the nation's top fighters risk only one or two invitational matches a year. Sometimes a winner requires six months of patching and recuperation. So long as he continues to win, his stud fee will be high and the prices for his pups will be outrageous, at least to the average dog lover.

It's possible to buy a good fighting dog, but again the price is high and the odds are risky. The breeders dominate the game, and they don't sell the best ones. Handled with care, meaning no more than one or two fights a year and handpicked opponents, a top dog has a career expectancy of about five years. Hardly any last beyond the age of seven. The will is still there, but the reflexes have slowed down, and the next fight may be the last one.

There's no such thing as retirement or a life of ease at stud for the veteran fighter who is over the hill. If not killed by a younger dog in the pit, he's soon destroyed by his owner. The veteran can never be a pet, of course, and his victor is the one who'll get the stud fees. So he's buried, and it is his owner who retires. A top fighting dog earns a fortune, and there's never been an owner of one who paid taxes on his winnings.

An average fight between top veterans will last from three to six hours. It usually ends with the loser dead or unconscious. A dog so exhausted that he cannot continue may turn away from his opponent. The rules of the game permit him a one-minute rest. Then he is forced back into battle, to kill or be killed. And all during the war, the shouts of the spectators are as savage as the snarls of the dogs.

Almost all of the important invitation matches are reported in detail by one or all of the fighting fancy's magazines. The most popular of these publications is *Pit Dogs,* and for a long time it was published in Washington, D.C. To the amazement of humane society agents assigned to investigate the reluctant publisher, it was discovered that the magazine was being produced on a lithographic press belonging to the Department of Defense. Further, the paper had been withdrawn from government supplies. All this was reported to a senator who had expressed sympathy for the humane movement. By the time he got around to investigating, the party under surveillance had removed all incriminating evidence and was no longer publishing at government expense. The postal authorities continue to deliver the magazine, of course, to all subscribers.

Pit Dogs and the fancy's other cultural publications do not term dogfighting as one of the last barbaric spectacles to which man has clung, but that's precisely what it is. Some of the spectacles of the Roman theater would be child's play in comparison.

Thus far, there's been no way to destroy or even curb this cruel, illegal sport. But the devotees are enthusiastic and ambitious, a couple of traits that may prove to be their undoing, or at least throw some confusion into the ranks. If rumors are true, then several leading breeders of fighting dogs will soon force their competitors out of business. They, supposedly, have managed to import, at great expense, several fighting dogs from China, by way of Hong Kong.

The Hong Kong version of the fighting dog would look more at home in a zoo than a pit. It breeds true to type, as it has for centuries, and its fighting assets include a thick, tough hide covered by bristles and teeth that resemble curved fangs. Heavier and leggier than the American fighters, they are strange, primitive-looking dogs, bred to kill and so talented in this specialty that their only equals in the animal world—pound for pound—are each other.

There are those who know the blood lovers and think they understand the mentality of our fighting dog breeders, and they believe the rumor. Americans are accustomed to having the best of everything, so why shouldn't our breeders want the best of the worst?

Humanitarians hope the rumor isn't true. They've seen so much unbelievable cruelty, they don't want to see any more.

Wildlife Games People Play 8

Licensed and unlicensed, about a seventh of our population engages in the ancient practice of hunting. Thirty million hunters, most of them men and boys, roam America and shoot at wild game, at innocent livestock, and often at each other. Hardly any of the thirty million have a real need for the meat, and a big percentage can't abide the taste of wild game anyway. And any hunter who does need meat would save time and money going to the marketplace.

So about all of the killing is needless. Still, it does get a man out into the fresh air where he can appreciate nature while destroying part of it, and where he can prove, to his own satisfaction, that he's superior to squirrels, rabbits and ducks. His ego is not even dented when the killed deer turns out to be a cow or a man. The cow or the man had no business acting and looking like a deer.

In the general context of cruelty to animals, however, the cruelty bestowed by the veteran hunter is of brief duration. The crack shot is the least of our sinners. Needless or not, the pain he imposes is soon over.

Unfortunately, the crack shot represents a minority among the thirty million. Despite the odds in his favor, the average hunter wounds more than he kills. Wildlife and conservation authorities agree that the wounded escape to die a lingering, painful death. The grand total of these suffering, destined-to-die creatures runs to about a billion every year. And the hunters make little or no attempt to find and relieve their wounded targets.

The sad truth is that most licensed hunters are not really qualified to hunt. Almost anyone of proper age and with a clean record can acquire a hunting license, and only a few states require that he have any knowledge at all about firearms. And everywhere it's assumed that the hunter knows a deer from a goat, or a goose from a swan, or a cow from a man. If it makes sense to require people to pass a driver's test before turning them loose on the highways, doesn't it make sense to require a hunter's test for those who want to hunt?

A secondary form of destruction which the hunter is responsible for—and from these deaths no one profits—is the casualties from wasted shotgun pellets. Scattered around lakes and ponds, loose shot is picked up by feeding birds. Three of the pellets will make a bird sick, four will make him sterile and five will kill him—another victim of carelessness.

Since it's no longer a matter of the survival of the fittest and few hunters really need the meat, psychologists reason that today's average hunter engages in his sport, if that's what it is, as an outlet for his instinct to kill. The hunter will deny this. He has a right to breathe fresh air and another right to enjoy nature's beauty, and if it weren't for hunting how could he take advantage of his rights? He could—the air and the beauty would be there even if he didn't carry a gun. But he doesn't.

In this status-conscious nation of ours, the deer represents status to most hunters. This wasn't always the case, but today the deer is the biggest wild animal most hunters hope to see, and he's available almost everywhere. If it sometimes seems that the deer population is keeping pace with the human explosion, that's because it is. Quite by accident, we have created an ideal environment for the deer. Our stripped forests and land usage have provided him with an abundance of the low, tender growth he prefers, and his predator enemies have been reduced in numbers or disappeared altogether. Unfortunately, the wolf has been replaced by man.

And wherever he roams, this graceful creature is threatened by the human predator. On the big, western ranges, the deer and all other forms of wildlife are shot and poisoned on a year-round basis so that cattle and sheep can find more to eat. These are public lands, leased to the ranchers by the Government, and the wildlife belongs to the taxpayers—not to the ranchers. The slaughter is unnecessary, since deer do not favor grass, and have been known to starve in the midst of it. The coyote and the hawk, to name just two of the also-persecuted, do not rob the cattle of grass, either. Yet, one branch of the Government sanctions these stupid range massacres, while, ironically enough, another spends millions trying to conserve our natural wildlife.

Washington, however, doesn't need help from the ranchers when it comes to protecting the range. Just recently, Yellowstone National Park rangers, aided by snowmobiles and helicopters, wiped out an entire herd of elk. The elk were supposedly destroying range land. Elsewhere, hunters were invited to help slaughter buffalo that had been driven within convenient shooting distance. There aren't many elk and buffalo left in this country, and our national parks are their last sanctuaries. Are the taxpayers supporting the ranchers? It looks that way.

The ranges aren't the only places where deer are needlessly slaughtered. The highway fatalities run into the thousands every month of the year. It's as if Detroit equips all cars with deer-finding radar. State highway departments do their best to help, but their best amounts to posting small DEER CROSSING signs in sixty-mile-per-hour speed zones. Only the manufacturers of home freezers benefit. Local police and state troopers are seldom short on venison.

In the suburbs, where residents pride themselves on being nature lovers, the deer live in a confused state. One man, an animal lover, will put out salt blocks for them. His next-door neighbor, a garden lover, will put out poison. And next door to him, a garden-hating, lazy hunter will plant corn in the hope of an easy shot at a prize buck. The law says he can protect his private property against damage, doesn't it? It does, and the same law usually says he should report his kill and turn the body over to the authorities. He doesn't.

Only in desperation does a suburbanite turn to the authorities. Such was the case of a new-home owner in California, who discovered that deer were nibbling on his shrubs. Seeking preventive measures, he called in the authorities, and they pointed out that his hillside site was smack in the middle of a deer trail that had existed for more than fifty years. The man wanted the entire herd of deer eliminated. A simple fence was the answer to his problem, but that was too expensive. The cost in deer lives was not.

Even deer lovers do injury to the deer. In summer and early fall, thousands of seemingly deserted fawns are discovered and brought home by gentle people who don't understand that the does are not irresponsible mothers and are never far away. Despite loving care and good intentions, most of the fawns die. Those who do survive are later released in the wilds. By this time the youngsters have no fear of man, and they walk right up to the first hunter they see.

At country clubs, where members delight in seeing deer on the fairways, the greenskeepers spread poison to eliminate the graceful creatures. The resultant corpses, even in the middle of summer, often lead to the conclusion that there are too many deer and that they are starving. It isn't true, of course, but the rumors help the hunters and game clubs and sporting goods manufacturers who are forever lobbying for longer open seasons and special seasons on does and fawns.

It is the hunter's self-helpful theory that there are always too many deer around and that a hard winter will cause many of them to die of starvation. In his opinion, shooting is more humane, and long before winter he is shouting for an extended open season, an increased bag limit, and no limitations as to sex and age. The fact that two out of every three deer he wounds are going to escape and die, and starve while dying—lower jaw shot away, leg broken, innards trailing, gangrene—does not cross his mind.

From time to time, state conservation departments have become convinced that the hunters are right: a deer would rather be killed than starve. Noting that the state is home to an overabundance of does, they announce a special "sexless" season to restore the balance of nature. It's silly reasoning, for in any given deer population, there are always more does than bucks. The buck is not a monogamist and considers five to fifteen does a proper family unit.

Not long ago, New York authorized a doe-and-fawn killing season in twenty-nine of its counties. The hunters had a wonderful time. Does fell by the thousands. Their fawns, three to six months old and all inexperienced in battle, fell with them.

The press was invited to cover the carnage. From one metropolitan newspaper: "Since I had reason to fear that the department's reports on the kill would be next to useless, I visited an official checking point until I was too disgusted and sorrowful to stand any more. I watched the shooters drive up with their bloody loads of fawns and does. For the most part, the fawns were concealed in rear compartments. The larger does were kept on the hoods of cars, a sure method of spoiling venison because of the heat."

The hunters were happy. They had achieved status. And the state officials were happy, because the herds had been reduced and the dead ones wouldn't starve. Oddly, all of the does and fawns killed were in splendid condition. None of the fawns were stunted, and many of the does were still in milk. If the hunters and the state authorities were right, then only the starving deer managed to escape the guns. All in all, the program was needless, thoughtless and cruel, so much so that it will probably be repeated in New York and other states.

The hunters are never satisfied, and thirty million voices constitute quite a lobby. They aren't satisfied in Maine, where the annual kill is better than forty thousand, or in Pennsylvania, where better than eighty-four antlerless deer were killed in one ten-hour day. About the only state where the deer aren't in danger is Delaware, where they were hunted into extinction fifty years ago. Any whitetail spotted there is a refugee from another state.

Ardent sportsmen insist that the thrill of hunting is in matching wits with a wild animal. If this is true, then they overestimate the intelligence of fawns, and they should somehow find a way to communicate with the adult deer, who having learned to live in harmony with man, and in close proximity most of the year, should be notified that on a given day man is no longer a friend. And the wealthy sportsmen, the captains of industry and other important individuals who belong to private game clubs must be pretty witless men, to judge by what they are choosing as opponents. They can sit on the clubhouse steps and bang away at deer or mallard or rabbits or grouse, all raised in captivity, all trusting men, and all released to be killed when the members are in the right mood and find the time convenient.

Since man has always hunted—originally for need and now for fun—the hunters cry that theirs is a noble sport. It may be "noble" in that at least the animal has a chance, whereas he doesn't in such areas as the slaughterhouse, the research laboratory, and the dogfight. He stands a chance not because he can outwit the hunter, but because so many hunters can't hit a barn door at fifty feet.

And to criticism of their favorite pastime, the hunters often point at the trappers and ask, "What about them? Just look at what they do to wildlife."

There aren't as many trappers as hunters, of course, and those who ply the trade don't consider it a sport. Except for the few who seek specimens to mount, the trapper, full-time or part-time, has money in mind. He concentrates on the furbearing animals whose pelts eventually grace the backs of men and women, among whom are sometimes leaders in the fight for stronger enforcement of the anticruelty laws. Most of them are unaware that trapping still exists. Either that, or they must assume that all fur is manufactured.

So it may come as news to them that trapping is still in existence. It's still a big business, it involves millions of suffering animals, and its methods are the same today as they were a hundred years ago. Alaska, of course, is the king of our trapping states.

The popular tool of the trade is the leg-holding trap. When the trap is sprung, its steel jaws close in a viselike grip on the animal's paw or leg. He experiences intense pain, and fights frantically to free himself. Usually, broken teeth result, but not infrequently the trapped victim will gnaw away until it has amputated its caught leg or paw, then escape to die on another day. But since the trapping business is successful, most of the trapped stay right where they are, destined to die from a combination of exposure, loss of blood, thirst and starvation, or to be put out of their misery by the returned trapper. In the latter case, the wait may be from a day to a week. Laws in some states do require that traps be checked daily. It is next to impossible to enforce those laws, as trappers know, and they don't like foul weather any more than the next fellow.

A version of the leg trap is used on water animals. As soon as its jaws close on any portion of the victim, down goes the trap. It doesn't make much difference how long the animal struggles—slow, painful drowning is his certain fate. No matter how many times he comes to the surface, he goes down an equal number of times, plus one.

The end is supposed to come quickly for the animal caught in the land trap known as the snare. This hoists the animal, dangles him by the neck, and causes strangulation. But it doesn't always work that way, and the victim may dangle by one leg for days until the trapper or starvation puts an end to him.

There are other, crueler traps in use, but none less cruel. The search for a truly humane trap has been going on for years and there's no hope in sight. The ideal trap would deal instant death through a blow or a shot. The entire fur industry, from trappers to manufacturers, remains most uninterested.

Bills to legislate humaneness into the trapping business are introduced at the federal level from time to time, but they never get out of committee. Somehow it seems more important to put a man on the moon than to relieve the needless suffering down here. And this suffering of furbearing animals in man's traps *is* needless today, for our fur farms can produce all the quality fur that's needed, and most farms kill humanely.

Our furbearers include the mink, beaver, muskrat, skunk, oppossum, weasel, wildcat, otter, several species of fox, fitch, lynx, marten, fisher, ermine, wolverine, wolf and bear. The complete list totals about forty, but the hunters and trappers have been so efficient that some are no longer in evidence south of Canada. Fortunately, many of the now rare species here are still abundant in Alaska. The per annum take there, however, is around 30 million pelts a year, and that yield won't last forever. Unless Alaska tightens its controls—a remote possibility at best—some of our furbearers will make their last stand in Canada, which also needs controls.

Whatever it is, and no man knows the exact figure, tens of millions of wild animals and birds are cruelly mistreated by red-blooded American hunters and trappers each year. And whatever that shocking total is, it still can't equal the toll excused in the name of pesticide programs. There's no disagreement between conservationists and humanitarians in this area. Both recognize the broad usage of pesticides as a national insanity, for by now the stacks of evidence are mountain high and plain for everyone to see. Pesticide control still amounts to pesticide miscontrol. In a given area, the target insect may be wiped out, but so is the wildlife: the animals, the birds and the fish, to say nothing of other living things that contribute to the balance of nature. And in the long run, man is poisoning himself, too.

DDT is the pesticide everyone knows by name. This is one of the many "persistent" pesticides, the lingering poisons, and it's used to fight almost everything, from gypsy moths to mosquitoes to Dutch elm disease. It is one of the many chlorinated hydrocarbons, related to the horrible nerve gases of World War I, and it can kill any organism possessing a nervous system. There are more potent pesticides available, but DDT is the most common in use, perhaps because its initials make it easier to remember.

DDT and more than 70,000 other chemical pesticides are available in this country, and sometimes it seems that all are being used on the same day. The main results are the poisoning of our wildlife and the poisoning of the vegetation and water they and our citizens consume.

As far back as 1963, the President's Science Advisory Committee (America was still talking about Rachel Carson's *Silent Spring*) advised that "elimination of the use of persistent toxic pesticides should be the goal." Despite this high-level study and recommendation, and the formation since (1964) of the Federal

Committee of Pest Control, composed of those departments utilizing pesticides (Agriculture, Defense, Health, Education and Welfare, and Interior), progress has been disappointing and slow. Indeed, some of the states have been far more active than Washington, but even at the state level, elimination of the dangerous pesticides continues to lag. Federal agencies, state agencies, local communities, private companies and private individuals (including just about every farmer) continue to spray away, poisoning our air and water and ground and nature in general, all to the detriment of our wildlife.

Why the continued mad use of pesticides? The manufacture of same is a billion-dollar business. The chemical companies want that market. Agriculture is more interested in immediate than long-term results in the battle with the pests, and private interests find the pesticides economical and convenient for their purposes. Together, they represent a formidable lobby, and this lobby has been able to dominate the scene and have its way despite the endless protests of ecologists, scientists, health authorities, conservationists, humane authorities, nature groups and millions of private citizens, all of them interested in guaranteeing a future in America for man, nature and wildlife.

Their cries have been heard in Washington, and today any new pesticide must be tested and registered by the Department of Agriculture before it can be marketed. This has cut down on the flow of new products, but it doesn't mean that the acceptable ones will be entirely safe. Presumably, if the pesticide's benefits outweigh its adverse side effects, it can be marketed. So the final decision becomes an arbitrary one. Even DDT could pass such a test, for there are those authorities who contend that the killing of mosquitoes is more important than the killing of everything else.

There's no reason to believe that the end of the indiscriminate usage of dangerous pesticides is in sight. But the day may come, and it could come with more speed if the nation's 30 million hunters woke up to the fact that pesticides are the reason millions of their targets don't live to see open season. By the time they awaken, some of their favorite game could be extinct or close to it.

Pesticides, of course, are a relatively new technique in our mad rush to murder all remaining wildlife. True, they weren't designed to endanger our wildlife, although that's what happened. As things stand now, it's a toss-up as to whether the havoc they cause is greater than a couple of other programs that were designed with destruction in mind: predator control and the bounty system.

Of the two, predator control probably does the most damage. It has been around for a long time, and its champions have almost always been farmers and ranchers. The long extinct passenger pigeon was one of our first official predators. Farmers fearing for the safety of their crops slaughtered the birds by the millions, surpassing even the market hunters. And it may be hard to believe, but the golden eagle wasn't safe in all states until recent years.

A predator is defined as a plunderer, and he can be

almost anything. Some states hold that skunks, porcupines and raccoons are predators, and thus should be destroyed on sight. Others don't agree, and apply that designation to the fox, gray squirrel and weasel. The states don't even agree upon the vanishing mountain lion and grizzly bear. Washington considers the diminutive prairie dog to be one of our mightiest plunderers; thus the black-footed ferret, who depends on the prairie dog and other destructive rodents, is close to extinction.

Rodents are plunderers, of course, as all farmers in all states will agree. The rat is the mightiest of our rodents. There's one of him for every two of us, and his damage is estimated at a billion dollars a year. We are losing the war with the rat, but Congress won't believe it. As recently as July 1967, it refused to vote additional funds to Harlem for rat control, and there may be more rats than people in Harlem.

It appears that Congress has unlimited faith in our main defense line against predators and rodents: the Branch of Predator and Rodent Control, Department of Interior. Obviously, Congress doesn't remember the 1964 Leopold Report: "The Branch of Predator and Rodent Control has developed into a semiautonomous bureaucracy whose function in many localities bears scant relationship to real need and less to scientific management."

Somehow, everybody is confident, this nation will find a way to win the war against the rat and his rodent allies. It will call for a change of tactics, and that's what worries the humanitarians. How long will it take for the changeover? Right now, because the BPRC lacks "scientific management," we are losing a more important war, the one dedicated to the preservation of this country's wildlife. Again, the Leopold Report: "Far more animals are being killed than would be required for effective protection of livestock, agricultural crops, wildland resources and human welfare."

Over the past two decades, the most effective weapon used against rodents and predators has been meat bait saturated with Compound 1080, a deadly poison. As in the case of deadly pesticides, 1080 sets off a chain of secondary killings. Thus the nightmare shared by humanitarians, conservationists and ornithologists alike: a poisoned rodent dies—a coyote finds him, eats him, and dies—a pair of condors find the coyote, eat him and die. It can happen, and it may have happened, and the condor is already on the verge of extinction. Less than a hundred of these giant birds remain, and the government and some states—the innocent taxpayers really—are endangering all of them. Meanwhile, private individuals and groups, none supported by tax dollars, are doing their best to save the condor. What the federal and state-level predator control programs are proving has already been proven: man is the worst predator of all, for he is capable of wiping out entire species within a short time; he has done so before and will do so again, unless he learns to control himself, which isn't likely.

Today, America's favorite predator target happens to be the coyote. In our western states, he is poisoned, trapped, shot, and destroyed in other cruel, more novel ways so that he won't plunder the herds of cattle and sheep on the ranges. The tax-supported coyote massacre has been going on now for about fifty years, and it shows no sign of abating, although for the past ten years or so it has been known that he's more of an asset than a liability. His normal meat diet consists of rodents, those destroyers of grains and grasses beloved by livestock. He is also a scavenger, and of course if he discovers a stillborn calf or lamb before the vultures do, he will not resist the temptation to dine. Nobody has ever witnessed him in the actual act of killing livestock, although it is presumed that a starving coyote might do so.

From a pioneer California cattleman: "It was an awful mistake to rid the country of the coyotes. I was raised where there were coyotes by the dozens and cows and calves on the range by the hundreds. I was out among those cattle every day in all kinds of weather and through calving time, and I never knew of a case of coyotes ever touching a calf." And from a prominent conservationist: "Whereas a coyote could kill a calf under unusual circumstances, they just don't regard them as prey. Coyotes are scavengers and will eat a dead calf, or an afterbirth. Thus, all too often, when a coyote is seen eating a dead animal, the conclusion is drawn that the coyote killed it. If a dead elephant were hauled onto the range and a coyote was found eating it . . ."

Largely by association, the coyote was condemned along with the wolf. When a pack of wolves left its kill, the coyote would move in to clean up the remains. Thus coyotes were suspected of being killers, too. Despite new knowledge, the old suspicion still persists in high quarters. So the falsely accused coyote is still persecuted, and apparently it has made him seek saner territory. He has drifted eastward in small numbers, and now his presence is not unusual in northern New York State. Just what damage he can do there is not quite clear, but he's shot on sight anyway.

The coyote is in no danger of extinction at the moment. But he's rarely found in some of the areas where he once roamed, and one of these days he'll be on view mostly in zoos, where he can't help in the war on rodents. His history will parallel that of the man-shy mountain lion, the predator who was fair game for so long because venison was his favorite dish. As mountain lions decreased, deer herds increased and so did deer destruction of young forest growth, tree farms, orchards and crops. It's the old story of the balance of nature. Upset it in one area, and a dozen new problems are born.

Predator control is an outgrowth of the old bounty system, and these days the new science of game management utilizes some of both. All three arts combined have but one notable victory to their credit: control of the wolf. The Massachusetts Bay Colony started an anti-wolf campaign back in 1630 by establishing the first American bounty of a penny per wolf. By the dawn of the twentieth century, the wolf was no longer a problem in the East, but his western cousin was thriving. His favorite source of fresh meat—the huge buffalo herds—had disappeared and he was concentrating on the new herds of cattle and sheep. This time, the bounty system didn't work. There were just too many wolves, and too many bounty hunters avoided shooting the females, to assure next year's crop of bounties. The cattle and sheep men shouted for help and help finally came from the Government. By 1925, hardly anyone could find a gray wolf, and the few spotted today are presumed to be wanderers from Canada or Mexico.

In the West, times haven't changed the attitudes of the livestock men who lease our federal ranges. Even those guilty of overcrowding the ranges with their cattle and sheep—a sure result of which is overgrazing and the resultant soil destruction—keep the war against wildlife in high gear. The ranchers feel that each blade of grass was created for their exclusive profit, and that only domestic livestock belongs on federal lands. There are always too many deer around, too many elk once in a while, plus the threatening rabbit, ground squirrel, and prairie dog. And seemingly all insects and birds are enemies, too. More often than not, Washington heeds the anxious calls of the livestock men and inaugurates another extermination program. It's never quite clear to the layman which federal agency or branch thereof is responsible for the massacre, and sometimes the responsible agency is unaware of what's going on until it's too late. Still, the men who lease the taxpayers' ranges have their way, and more of the taxpayers' wildlife is destroyed.

But in the area of needless destruction of wildlife, Washington does not stand alone. More than half our states continue to pay respect to the bounty system, in the fairly civilized East as well as the wild West. As in the case of predator control, the states do not agree as to just who the enemies are. The prairie dog is a fine example. He is not a predator, and nobody has ever been able to prove what harm he does (if any), but there is a bounty on him in several western states. It's the same with the red fox in some eastern states. The farmers now know that he's more friend than foe, but the hunters claim the fox devours too many game birds. This claim has been disproven many times. It's a rare fox who dines more than occasionally on fowl, but every chipmunk dreams of dining on game bird eggs during the nesting season, and there are no bounties on chipmunks, the favorite diet of fox. Until recently, the bald eagle was bountied in Alaska. The bird will eat salmon, and the commercial fishermen didn't like that. The hawk, weasel, skunk and raccoon do not trouble fishermen, but they annoy somebody, and all bring bounty payments in several states.

The bounty system calls for the delivery of evidence before payment, and nobody cares how the evidence is obtained, be it by shooting, trapping, poisoning, clubbing or stoning. The young and the old pursue this activity as a sport, for one can't make a living at bounty hunting these days. Roll all the bounty payments of all the states together, add the innumerable local programs (as when skunks or rabbits or squirrels are suspected of carrying rabies), and the grand total comes to about half a billion dollars in bounty payments a year. The programs are underwritten by the taxpayer, of course, and most of the creatures on the bounty lists do more good than harm. No single authority has come along to prove otherwise.

In this day and age, the bounty system is no more nor less than an arm of politics, and politics isn't concerned with our wildlife. There may be times when the reduction of a species is necessary, but those times are few and are best handled by the experts in ecology, conservation and management. Our wildlife belongs to all of the people, although the hunters and trappers and farmers and ranchers don't seem to see it that way. Thus far, we have failed miserably in conserving our wildlife, and the needless cruelties we extend to them exceed, or at least equal, the foolish brutalities we impose upon our domestic friends.

If our grandchildren are going to see and appreciate some of the creatures who were intended to inhabit America with us, then it's high time—not too late, but almost so—for all interested citizens to get behind some group that is fighting to maintain a balance of nature and seeking ways to inject morality and common sense and kindness into the bloodstreams of our lawmakers.

The cruelties we inflict upon our domestic animals in the name of profit is bad enough, but there's no excuse at all for what we're doing to our wildlife. What we need, obviously, is a federal control program for the human predator.

The Sport of Kings 9

HUGE INVESTMENTS AND GREAT, RESPECTED NAMES are involved in horse racing. For those reasons, the knowing find it inconceivable that so little attention is paid to the welfare of the animals who keep the show going: the thoroughbreds.

All thoroughbreds have a common birthday: January First. Thus a horse foaled any time after that date is presumed to be a year old on the first day of the new year. It's possible, then, for a day-old thoroughbred to be a year old as far as the racing authorities are concerned: Foaled on December 31, 1960—one year old the next day, January 1, 1961—and three years old on January 1, 1963 and eligible to qualify for such races as the Kentucky Derby.

So some of the racing three-year-olds are nowhere near that age, and all of them, even those legitimately aged three, had to start their training at a very tender age and race as two-year-olds. Time after time, while they're still growing and their bodies aren't ready for the task, the youngsters are forced and whipped into expending the final ounce of physical effort. It's a strenuous life, hard on muscle and bone and heart. Little wonder that the thoroughbred's racing life is so short, or that a sound horse in any flat race, anywhere, is a rarity. The winning horse always appears sound, especially if he's setting a track record, but the fact is that he's in just a little better shape than the others. "Doctoring" is the name of the game, and many a veterinarian would be a poorer man today if he lacked the ability to get a horse "up" for a particular race. The scratches represent horses who haven't responded.

The general public recognizes the fact that thoroughbreds are delicate animals, subject to all sorts of injuries, and believes that this is because of fine breeding. This is nonsense, of course. The racing thoroughbred is a delicate animal here in America because he's asked to do too much too early in life. This is known by everyone associated with horse racing in America: the Jockey Club, the owners, the breeders, the trainers, the veterinarians, the sporting press, and all track officers, to name a few. The early training and racing is abuse of the highest order, but those who criticize horse racing for this very reason are in turn criticized by those whose fortunes are tied to horse racing. They insist that horse racing is honest, although that has nothing to do with the accusation of abuse. They point out that tax dollars are important to the economy, and that has nothing to do with the subject either. With these arguments, they cloud the real issue, and to date the trick has worked. And as for doctoring, they say, doesn't everybody know that drugs used to stimulate a horse or kill pain have been outlawed?

It is true that horses no longer go to the post aided by morphine, heroin, cocaine, strychnine, caffein and codeine. What everybody outside of racing doesn't know is that there are 350 more available drugs, and scores of them cannot be detected by the routine saliva and urine tests used at the tracks.

Racing has steadily expanded over the years. The competition for the racing dollar and the tax dollar has meant more races per day, more days of racing per year, in some cases year-round racing, and it is the horses that suffer. There are few sound racehorses—hard tracks, lack of proper rest, unsound breeding, overuse of young horses, poor trainers and exercise riders add up to a large percentage of horses to which the performance of their "function" is unnecessarily cruel and debilitating.

A New Jersey veterinarian: "If we scratched all the sore horses going to the post, there would be no racing at all. Easily 75 percent of all horses running have something wrong with them. The other 25 percent are perfectly sound, but have one drawback as racers—they can't run fast."

The late, beloved Damon Runyan: "I once read that horse racing is for the purpose of improving the breed of horses. That strikes me as very funny, because I know that of all the thousands of race horses in the United States, there are not as many as a hundred, including the proudest of stake horses, that are completely sound."

The stake races represent the big money. This is where the two- and three-year-olds run their hearts out, and a few win fame and fortune, become household words, and are suddenly retired. The news stuns millions of admirers, but they are soothed by the noble words of the retired thoroughbred's owner: "The time to retire is when you're on top. Money isn't everything." Translated, that means the young horse's crippled legs wouldn't carry him through another race, and he was lucky to win by a nose the last time out. Bowed tendons mean he's through as a runner, but firing or working blisters, both extremely painful cures, might strengthen his legs and make him useful as a stud. His offspring will bring top prices, and some may win top purses if they can still run after an adolescence of ruptured ligaments, fractured sesamoids, cracked hoofs, bony growths and other avoidable ailments.

Since only three horses per stake race are in the money, most of the runners in the big time do not win enough to pay for their oats. They move down to the claiming races, sinking lower in class as age, old infirmities and new ailments combine to slow their speed. They move from owner to owner, barn to barn, and track to track. Now it's a case of much doctoring and automatic response to the whip. For many a thoroughbred, relief doesn't come until his leg breaks. The relief is a bullet between the eyes. It's a common occurrence at the small tracks, where the former greats are still asked to race. And it isn't unknown at the big tracks, where the still-great race.

There wouldn't be any horse racing without horses, of course, but there's nobody around to represent them. Owners, jockeys, trainers and handlers have their protective groups, but the horse's welfare depends on his owner's conscience. But others outside of racing did come forward not long ago with a sort of equine-medicare plan for disabled and retirement-age thoroughbreds. The sponsoring group would pay an agreed sum for each horse, then care for the horses for the rest of their days. There are sentimentalists in the racing world, and they thought highly of the plan before learning that most of the financing would have to come from racing itself—perhaps a few pennies deducted from each winning purse. That was the end of that plan.

Of all the groups affiliated with horse racing, only the Thoroughbred Racing Association has shown an active interest in the welfare of horses. It, at least, has urged its member tracks to be aware of fire hazards and take the necessary precautions against fires. Many of the tracks have responded, and at them, an owner can relax and rest assured that his horses occupy fire-resistant quarters. But all tracks aren't members, and stable fires continue to claim an average of over a hundred thoroughbred lives a year. For three decades now, most of the fires have occurred at small, local tracks, such as the ones at fairgrounds. The country is dotted with these firetraps called stables, and all seem to be immune from local fire laws and building codes. There's no major reform in sight, and no reason to believe that there will ever be. Somehow, politics and racing go hand in hand. The old barns will remain unimproved until they fall down or burn down, and the latter is the likelier prospect. This year and next, and for a good many more years, at least a hundred horses will die in their flames.

And not all of the horse owners will be sorry. As insurance company records prove, arson fires are not unknown at the small tracks. The man who races a string of horses isn't always a millionaire, and overhead is expensive. If he's supporting consistent losers and they happen to be insured, a fire can look like an easy means to a fresh bankroll and a fresh start. It seems so simple, for many a small track barn lacks electricity, and it's easy to tip a kerosene lamp. The only victims are the horses, and the horses belonging to others, too.

Some are wealthy enough to deny it, but all those associated with horse racing are in it for the money, and the thoroughbreds are a necessary means to that end. The same cannot be said for that other large group of horse devotees, or the ladies and gentlemen of the horse-show set. They think of themselves as true horse lovers, and perhaps most of them are. They certainly spend vast sums on their horses, and their winnings—when they happen to own a winning horse—amount to only ribbons and trophies, neither negotiable for cash. So it would be difficult to accuse the horse-show set of being inspired by the profit motive. If there are blue bloods in the horse world, members of the horse-show set are the bluest.

Yet some of them treat their four-footed prides and joys in the strangest manner. Consider any owner of a Tennessee Walking Horse. The horse's rear legs carry most of his weight and he's all high action in front. As he moves along, his forelegs reach out and his front hoofs seem to barely touch the ground. Roughly speaking, the gait is inherited. But for show purposes, the natural gait must in most cases be enhanced, and this requires training by man.

Among the popular training aids are burning chemicals, chains, misshapen shoes and weights of up to six pounds on each foot. Soreing or tenderizing the forefeet is almost a must, and the methods include the application of painful chemicals to the hoofs and the rubbing of salt into a cut placed at the cornet band (in the flesh and just above the hoof). A stubborn horse may require "chaining," or the wrapping of chains around his legs so that, in attempting to throw them off, he'll exaggerate his steps as he walks. And he'll want to gain freedom from those chains, since they are wrapped around sore areas, and the sores have been rubbed raw with irritating salves.

Chains are forbidden in the show ring, of course, but decorative boots are allowed. It's all the same to the horse. As he gaits along, the boots slide up and down, rubbing against the sore spots and aggravating his pain. The boots hide the raw, sore spots, but the blood often seeps out into plain view. Judges manage to overlook this evidence, perhaps because most judges were once trainers and understand that cruelties, while forbidden by show rules, are a necessity.

Horse-show rules do forbid all the practices mentioned above. The owners, or horse lovers, are aware of the rules, but their trainers interpret them in their own fashion. Indeed, some of the land's top trainers have developed their biggest winners by starting them as young colts. If the cruelties are inflicted at an early age, the developing youngster will throw his weight back and keep his rump down, and his spine will grow accordingly. That's the theory, and veteran trainers swear that it works.

Obviously, reform and policing are necessary. The responsibility for both would seem to be the clear duty of the Walking Horse Association, but don't tell that to former Governor Buford Ellington of Tennessee. He spent six long years urging the president of the Association to ban the cruel practices, but nothing happened.

Something could happen, however, for Senator Joseph D. Tydings of Maryland has introduced a bill in Congress that could bring relief to the famous walking horse. Trainers in particular should be interested in his introductory remarks:

> In recent months the nation's attention has been focused upon inhumane treatment of domestic dogs and cats. We were all sickened by the article in *Life* magazine which showed intolerable cruelty to dogs in, I am ashamed to say, Baltimore, Maryland. All animal lovers are gratified that the House and Senate have held hearings on the problems of dognapping and humane treatment of laboratory animals.
>
> There is another problem of cruelty to animals which has recently come to my attention, which also requires corrective legislation and which the pending bills do not cover. I refer to the widespread abuse of the beautiful Tennessee walking horse for the purpose of affecting its natural gait.
>
> Most of us at some time in our lives have attended a horse show and thrilled to these magnificent animals proudly prancing around a show ring. The Ten-

nessee walking horse's stride is long; its front feet barely touch the ground. As a matter of fact, our President's favorite mount, when he is on the ranch, is one of this fine breed.

Unscrupulous owners and trainers of Tennessee walking horses have discovered that if the horse's front feet are sore he will lift them quickly from the ground, shift his weight to his sound hindquarters, and take the much desired long-striding step. This soreing usually is done by using chains or tacks inside the quarter boot or by applying a burning agent to the pastern, the area just above the hoof. These agents vary, but the most common are an oxide of mercury salve, known as "creeping cream," and an oil of mustard mixture, called "scooting juice." Another technique, recently adopted, is to drive a nail into the tender part of the hoof. This is more difficult to detect, but equally effective and painful.

These despicable practices are condemned by responsible organizations and by some State Legislatures. The Tennessee Walking Horse Breeders' and Exhibitors' Association of America officially prohibits the soreing of Tennessee walkers for show purposes, and published a notice, effective September 15, 1964, announcing that "due to flagrant violations by exhibitors" it will take disciplinary action. The American Horse Show Association also prohibits the showing of horses "equipped with artificial applications, such as leg chains, wires or tacks, blistering or any other cruel and inhumane devices."

My own State of Maryland and other States, including Tennessee, have statutes that prohibit the showing of horses that have been tortured or cruelly treated.

I regret to say, Mr. President, that the rules and

> regulations of the horse associations and even the State statutes have been more honored in the breach than in the observance. An article by Alice Higgins in the January 11 issue of *Sports Illustrated,* a story by Mr. George Coleman in the January 6, 1966, edition of the New York *World Telegram and Sun,* and statements by Mr. H. M. Oler of the American Humane Association and Mrs. Pearl Twyne of the Virginia Humane Association, all attest to the fact that the deplorable practice of soreing Tennessee walkers is widespread.

The bill has been drawn as follows:

> It shall be unlawful for any person to transport, or ship, or cause to be transported or shipped, to receive in interstate commerce any horse whose legs or hoofs have been made sore, after the date of enactment of this Act, for the purpose of affecting or altering the natural gait of such horse. The legs or hoofs of a horse shall be considered to have been made sore if chains have been used in a manner designed to break the skin surface of the horse, or if a blistering agent has been applied internally or externally on the horse, or if a chemical agent, or tacks, nails, or wedges have been used on the horse, or if any other method or device has been used which causes intense physical pain to the horse when walking, trotting or running. The fine is designated at $500 or imprisonment of six months or both and the Secretary of Agriculture is authorized to enforce the legislation.

The bill is still a bill, not a law, and it can be assumed that Senator Tyding's remarks lost him a few votes in Maryland, where the horse-show set is very strong and Tennessee Walking Horses are held in high esteem. And he would have lost even more votes had he seen fit to attack the common practice of tail setting, an extremely painful operation that results, when successful, in an arched or "waterfall" tail. It's found on the walker and other show horses, and represents the horse lover's artistic improvement on nature. The horse knows how to carry his tail and how to use it, but many a horse lover thinks differently. After all, humans are more intelligent animals. So it has become fashionable to give the show horse a tail that doesn't look like a horse's tail. It is achieved by cutting the strong flexor muscles at the base of the tail. The tail is then bent up at a right angle, tightly bandaged, and held in place by a mechanical device until the wounds heal. The healing process takes weeks, and the horse is in pain every minute of the time. Once the wounds have healed, the chances are about even that the tail will set up perfectly straight and show the proper arch. If the tail slants to one side, the operation and healing periods are repeated. A horse may spend painful months undergoing one operation after another, and never achieve the desired tail.

But even after a successful operation, the arched tail doesn't stay in perfect arch all of the time. Every day, between shows and just before shows, the tail must be kept in "set," or in its braces. During each such beauty treatment for his tail—which lasts hours at a stretch—the horse feels pain.

Under existing anticruelty laws, tail setting was outlawed in New York and several other states within the past several years. But the operation is still performed in New York and all the other states, and every horse show in every state has its representation of arched tails. And apart from the shows, many a hack brings a higher price because his tail has been set.

The horse lovers do not consider the arched tail important on their jumpers. The jumper's task is to jump, and personal beauty will not sway the judges. So he escapes tail setting and learns to live instead with an instrument known as the "tack-pole." The pole is about ten feet long, and quite often it is studded with sharp nails or spikes. It is employed as a training aid, and its purpose is to make the horse jump higher than he feels like jumping.

As the horse closes in on the practice jump and gathers himself, the pole wielder, who is standing by, bangs the pole against the horse's legs or belly. Encouraged by the sudden pain, the horse soars higher than is his wont. If he's a thinking horse, he won't have to be banged by the pole every time. After a while, he'll note the pole and jump higher to avoid the pain.

Some trainers insist that the poling method is all right as far as it goes, but it doesn't go far enough. So they utilize the "tack-rail," which becomes the top rail of the jump. If the jumper doesn't clear the jump with room to spare, he rips both his belly and his legs.

The tack-rail method has modified forms, such as holding a bamboo pole above the top rail, or stretching a thin, almost invisible wire above and across the rail. The wire is used most frequently in teaching a horse that he'd better raise his hind legs higher than usual. It has caused many a horse to somersault, and broken legs and necks have resulted. A horse's underpinnings are his weakest point, and a break or fracture above the ankle means he's crippled for life. When this occurs, he is usually destroyed.

The practice of poling has been declared illegal in several states, and elsewhere it and railing can be prosecuted under anticruelty laws. But both training methods remain fairly common, for it would take an army to patrol the private estates of horse lovers, and all of them are loyal to their trainers. A good trainer is hard to find, and the good ones produce the best jumpers. But they are not creative men, in the sense that they have not created painless training methods, or found jumping inducements that safeguard a horse's legs.

Almost as appalling as what happens to show horses is the story of their sisters in the drug industry:

There wouldn't be any story if it weren't for estrogen, the widely used female sex hormone. The most important basic in the commercial production of estrogen is derived from the urine of pregnant mares. Some ten thousand mares are responsible for an annual five million dollars of estrogen sales.

A few drug manufacturers maintain their own facilities for mares, but most contract with farmers. Hence the term "mare farms," where most of the ten thousand mares are "in residence," a condition that humanitarians regard as slavery of the lowest possible sort.

The drug manufacturers have been somewhat reticent about revealing statistics, but there are approximately 300 mare farms in operation today, and there will be more next year, since the demand for estrogen is on the increase. On a large percentage of the current farms, conditions are atrocious.

Housing consists of old, flimsy, unheated, wooden structures. The removal of droppings is occasional at best. The mares stand on several feet of dung, some with their rumps bumping the shed roof. The stench is unbearable for humans.

For the entire year of her pregnancy, the mare occupies the same stanchion or stall. She never sees sunlight and often lives in complete darkness. She is fed an unnatural diet, and sometimes must be force-fed with fluids. The feeding is the only attention she receives. There's never any exercise or grooming. And during every moment of her pregnancy, she wears a special harness that's designed to collect her urine.

Her only relief comes when she foals, and the relief is brief. Seven days later, the foal is removed from her side and she is bred again. Then it's back to the stall and the harness. She lives her life this way.

There's no place for the foals on the farms. But they are dividends for the farmers, and are sold or auctioned for whatever they'll bring. If eight or ten babies show up at a livestock auction, it's reasonable to assume that a mare farm is somewhere nearby. If one of the foals is in good health, that's a miracle. They, too, are neglected by the contract farmers, a class of men who have never heard of Albert Schweitzer. That great man's works should be required reading for every man who runs a mare farm, and for every officer of every drug company concerned with estrogen.

What all of them need is a hormone that induces reverence for life.

The Wild and the Worn 10

THE WILD HORSE—THE MUSTANG OF AMERICA'S WESTern folklore—has inhabited the ranges of this continent since the early sixteenth century, when his ancestors fled their Spanish masters for the freedom of the wild. But although he has existed in his truly wild state for three centuries, he is descended from a domesticated beast, so the purists refer to him as feral. Because of this little matter of definition, he has never qualified for the protection granted other forms of wildlife by the United States Wildlife Service.

And he has suffered from this lack of protection. A century ago, millions of his kind roamed the Great Plains, with the largest herd concentrations in Texas and Montana. As the West was settled and the land was fenced, they retreated to the Rockies and beyond. The Indians caught a few to replenish their own riding stock, and the only critics were ranchers whose mares decided to join the wild herds. Then, at the turn of the century, the mustang became a thing of value. The Boer War was on, the British needed horses, and the purchasing agents didn't care if the horses were broken or not. Mustangs were rounded up by the thousands and sold to the British.

After that, the herds weren't bothered much for fifteen years. Then, during the First World War, the

Army rounded up tens of thousands for use as cavalry mounts and dray horses for both our own forces and those of our European allies. It was the beginning of the end for the big, wild herds. In the 1920's, the demand for cheap horsemeat soared. It was used as an additive for chicken feeds, and later canned for dog and cat food, and for the animals on fur farms. Horsemeat was also processed for human consumption, mostly for export. The mustang became the beloved of the profit makers. He was free for the taking, and there were plenty of takers.

Then, as if he wasn't having enough trouble just staying alive, he had to face official Washington. The ranchers didn't want to share their leased ranges with the wild horses. Overgrazing was the cry. So the Bureau of Land Management, the Forest Service and the Bureau of Indian Affairs joined hands in common cause: remove the wild horses from federal land, the only home remaining for the horses.

In effect, the federal decision to "remove" meant "destroy." Thus, in one of history's largest roundups, over ten thousand mustangs were "removed" from the Navajo Indian Reservation. Another ten thousand were shot on Arizona's San Carlos Indian Reservation, and a thousand more in Sitgreaves National Forest. Additional thousands went to their death in Montana, and at least four thousand in Oregon. But the record was set in Nevada: over 100,000 wild horses went to their doom, although the Government preferred to think of them as feral horses. Great areas of land were covered in the program, but the horses never had a chance. They were herded by airplane into convenient locations and caught or shot in traps. And during all this time, a period of almost twenty years, private interests were also hunting down wild horses for the canneries. The market price averaged out at six cents per pound.

Today, there are less than twenty thousand wild horses in the West, mostly in Nevada, New Mexico, Oregon, Utah and California. Texas and Montana together, where millions once roamed, can't claim a thousand. Anywhere, a herd of twenty-five is a big herd today.

Still, the mustang is lucky to be around at all, and he owes his good fortune to one woman. She's Velma B. Johnston of Reno, known to the true horse lovers and humanitarians who supported her efforts as "Wild Horse Annie." Thanks to her, Congress finally (1959) got around to passing a bill that forbids the use of motorized equipment in the hunting of wild horses. This made things difficult for the exterminators, who depended so much on the airplane and the helicopter, but it didn't discourage them. Ranchers still take their toll, and the Bureau of Land Management experts are still thinning out the herds on federal ranges. And although the big profits aren't there anymore, private interests still hunt the wild horses and deliver their victims to the rendering plants.

The methods haven't changed much, except that the herding is done on land and not from the air. Once trapped, the horses are roped, tied and dragged up a loading ramp into a truck. The truck heads for the slaughter-house, and it doesn't make much difference if they arrive there dead or alive. They'll be converted into chicken or pet food in any case.

But roping, tying and dragging aren't the only activities at an average roundup. Little tricks of the trade include sewing a mustang's nostrils together so that he can't get enough air to race away, and slitting the throats of colts so that they can't run very far. A huge tire at the end of a rope acts as an anchor and soon tires a horse. These minor abuses were in evidence at a Government-sponsored roundup in Wyoming, and may have inspired the current clamor in that state for protection of the wild horse. To date, and again the credit goes to Mrs. Johnston, Nevada has the only law designed to protect the mustang. But Wyoming looks promising, and there's very strong protectionist sentiment in Utah and California. So state-level action rather than federal action may save the wild horse from extinction. Meanwhile, the abuse of the animal continues.

His opposite number—the horse who never had a chance to turn wild, or feral—is the horse-for-hire found in the riding stable, the last stop before conversion into pet food or mink fodder. Usually his best days are behind him. He's a reject from the racing or show worlds, or he was never much of a saddle horse anyway. And now, in his final years, he's supposed to carry people on his back until his legs will no longer support him.

As small businesses go, the average riding stable is among the most sordid. These stables flourish all over the country, and checking on the welfare of the horses would require the full time of all the local humane societies in the United States. Unfortunately, the societies can't spare that much time, and the stable owners are well aware of the fact.

With a bare minimum of exceptions, the stables are housed in dilapidated old sheds, barns or buildings useless for any other purpose. Too many are firetraps, and most communities exempt them from building codes. The vermin outnumber the horses, and most of the stables are disease incubators. From normal safety and health viewpoints, at least half of the stables should be closed.

To break even, or to show a profit, the stables operate as if there were an unwritten code of mistreatment. The horses are bought as cheaply as possible and then are used as much as possible. Meanwhile, overhead must be kept to a minimum. The business is largely seasonal in many parts of the country, and in any climate foul weather keeps the action down. With those risks in mind, who can blame a stable owner for shorting his charges on proper rations, shoes, and vetting? And since maximum usage per horse unit is the yardstick for success, who can fault the owner for sending out his horses time after time, with no cooling-off period in between? After all, it might rain tomorrow.

Saddle sores are the emblems of the stable horses. They are tender and very painful, especially when weight is applied from above. Pads and sponges under the saddle blanket make them a little less painful, although they don't help the healing. The owners are grateful for sponges, since they can keep a horse going all day. The horse is a business liability when he's standing around in a stall.

While the rate-per-hour varies around the country, the horse for hire earns his keep if he is hired out twice a week. Unless the owner is an idiot and is attempting to do business in a ghost town, all of his horses should show a weekly profit. Over the past twenty years, hacking has enjoyed a tremendous popularity boom, and there's no decline in view. More newcomers enter the activity every year, more by far than golf and tennis combined. Children love to ride; just donning a riding habit makes the stoutest woman feel like Miss America; and it's cheaper to hire a horse than own one. This boom doesn't help the horses, but it explains why more rental stables pop up every year.

It doesn't help the horses because the newcomers are inexperienced, and they ride off with a minimum of instructions, if any. With safety in mind, the novice is usually assigned to the oldest, weariest horse available. And the novice, especially if he's a youngster, has speed in mind. So horse usage is quite often misusage, and nobody really cares. Not the rider, not the stable owner, and not the next rider nor the next.

The owner's problem of what to do with his horses during the off-season is usually solved by farming them out to individuals who use them as they see fit. For the humans involved, it's a convenient arrangement, but the horses often find themselves worse off than back in the stable. Overriding, inadequate rations, lack of shelter for horses who have not grown winter coats, and complete disregard for shoeing and simple care are among the abuses perpetrated by the uninformed. Many a horse must be happy to get back to the dismal riding stable when spring rolls around, if he's able to keep alive that long.

The riding-stable owners aren't the only ones dedicated to the farming-out policy. It's popular with resort owners and summer-camp operators, and in such cases it can be considered akin to a humane act. Their horses, at least, have a chance for a little human attention and care. At season's end, too many resorts and camps simply turn their horses loose and hope that most can be found before the new business season begins. Some of the neglected horses are sure to die and some may be stolen, but such losses are meaningless. The owners will find more cheap horses to replace the missing ones.

Then there's a third fate for the worn-out saddle horses nobody wants to feed through the winter. This is the mink farm, or the end of the trail for the horses. Mink are fond of horsemeat, and the mink farmers are ever on the alert for a cheap source of supply. They find it wherever thrifty horse owners are anxious to cut down on overhead. The farmers will go as high as a penny-per-pound on the hoof, and that averages out to about ten dollars a horse. And here we run into another of man's inconsistencies: the average fur farmer now kills his charges in a humane manner, but he's a barbarian when it comes to slaughtering the food horses, and makes the ritual slaughtering practices look like child's play.

So that's the way it goes for the tired saddle horses from the dreary stables, the fancy resorts, and the high-tuition summer camps. About half a million face an uncertain future when the business season ends, and half of those don't live through the winter. Those are the rewards for accepting overwork and abuse while showing a profit for owners. If only some of the pleasure riders derive could be transferred to the horses they ride.

There's nothing new in the American mania for mistreating the horse. He's been the object of abuse from the time when he was first domesticated, and his whole story is linked with certain ironies. Take away the horse, and much of world history would have to be rewritten. Without him, we might still be trying to settle America. Because of him, or more so than any other animal, the humane movement was started in this country, yet to date he's received less relief from cruelty than most other animals, domestic or wild. And that includes some of those favored ones who entertain us via television and the films.

Codeville, U.S.A. 11

It may come as a surprise to millions of film-goers, but the motion-picture industry does have a code. It is the Motion Picture Production Code and it governs what can and what cannot be shown in American-made films. Questionable morals, religious themes, and cruelty to children and animals are some of the many touchy subjects it covers. Films made by members of the Motion Picture Association of America must meet the code's standards and abide by the decisions of its administrators.

The code has been around for a long time. Right from its inception, it didn't approve of cruelty to animals. But the measure of cruelty depended on the entertainment value of the act. If the public enjoyed watching the cavalry charge and seeing the horses fall all over the battlefield, then the resultant broken legs and necks did not constitute cruelty—it was entertainment.

For too many years, the code was absolutely meaningless. Despite mounting criticism from the humane movement, Hollywood continued to treat its animal actors in a cruel manner. So long as the desired effect was achieved, anything was permissible. The film-going public, of course, remained innocent of what was going on behind the scenes.

Then, in 1939, a film company on location in Missouri went a little too far. In the interests of entertainment, two horses were shoved down a greased chute and sent flying over a cliff. From there they dropped seventy-five feet into the waters of a lake. One of the horses was killed, but the producer had what he wanted on film, and news of the feat was released to the press. It brought more than 50,000 letters of disapproval, plus an intensified investigation of Hollywood's treatment of animals by societies engaged in the humane movement. On horses alone, the findings were shocking.

If a film has more than a few horses in its cast, it is almost an iron rule that it will have as many as possible falling to the ground. And it *is* the iron rule for such scenes as cavalry charges, Indians encircling burning covered wagons, and the chase that leads to the climax. So horses must fall. Whether they get to their feet again or not is and always has been unimportant in the Hollywood view.

It takes a long time, but it is possible to train a galloping horse to fall on command. These "falling horses" are available for films, but the supply is limited. There never have been more than ten around at one time. They have no liking for their specialty and one fall a day is about all the jarring they'll tolerate. The fall must be on prepared, cushioned ground so that the faller won't be hurt. The rental price is high. So the ten horses don't work very often.

With a strong stunt man in the saddle, a producer doesn't need a trained falling horse. Any horse will do. If the stunt man has rodeo experience behind him, he knows just how to shift his weight, jerk the reins, twist the head and force the running horse to the ground.

Of course, stunt men are expensive, too, and there aren't enough of them around anyway when horses must fall in quantity. Then it's simpler and cheaper to stretch out a cable and trip the running horses. Or, just to put a little variety into the entertainment, a few dozen pits can be dug and camouflaged with light brush.

But best and surest of all is the "Running W." Hobbles are attached to the horse's front legs, and a cable is attached to the hobbles. The other end of the cable runs to a metal stake. The cable length is determined by the position of the cameras. Now the horse is set in motion, and at the desired point the cable pulls his legs from under him and he goes head over hoofs to the ground. When 1,200 pounds of horseflesh go smashing to the ground, something has to give, and it's seldom the ground. The least the horse can suffer is shock, bruises and extreme fright. Broken bones and a bullet are likelier. The film footage never reveals the aftereffects, of course.

The trip wire and the pitfall and the Running W were all common film practices at the time the two horses were pushed over the cliff in Missouri, but the pushing incident brought on the pressure, and by 1940 the film industry was ready to revise its code insofar as it pertained to cruelty to animals.

The new code came too late to stop the release of that particular film, but it did take giant steps of promise concerning animal welfare in films. It outlawed the trip wire, pitfall, and Running W by stipulating, "There shall be no use of any contrivance or apparatus for tripping or otherwise treating animals in an unacceptably harsh manner." That ruling should have saved the lives of thousands of horses by now. Unfortunately, some producers don't recognize the Running W when they see it. The device is still in use today.

Thus, the code promised that animals used in films would not be subjected to harsh treatment. It's possible that this terminology has been a deterrent to some cruelty, but it certainly hasn't stopped it. Jungle films, wherein two beasts tear each other to shreds, are not regarded as harsh treatment of animals. This is always excused as educational entertainment, showing two natural enemies having at each other, even when the combatants are natives of different continents.

But best of all was the new code's permission of the presence on the set of a representative of the American Humane Association. He was to oversee the use of all animals in a given film, from script to shooting to final footage, and either suggest the elimination of dangerous or harmful actions or determine that protective measures were taken. That was the agreement in 1940, and that's the way it is today, and the humane agent is almost as powerless today as he was in 1940. To simulate death scenes, animals are still being given doses of anesthetic, and dying as a result. To achieve the desired result, directors are still using chutes, electric shock, wires and other cruel devices. Rodeo scenes use rodeo livestock and the livestock receives rodeo treatment. Hollywood's humane agent has one of the world's most frustrating jobs.

Hollywood's disrespect for its own code was revealed to the fullest quite recently, when *The Brave One* was filmed. This was made by an American company, a member in good standing of the film industry and thus bound by its code. The film honored the bullfight, and from any animal lover's point of view it had to be the goriest film ever made. It wasn't the first bullfight film, but it was the first in color, and those who saw the film knew that the blood was real. As bullfights go, this was an authentic film, and its cruelties to animals were exposed not as barbaric actions, but as honorable ones.

At no time—from start to finish—was there any consultation with any member of the humane movement. In further defiance of his own code, the producer disregarded completely all the stipulations pertaining to animals. And then, in one of history's great examples of mental gymnastics, the producer suggested that the film be made the symbol for the national "Be Kind To Animals Week," for the story line did include a boy who loved a bull. The suggestion was not accepted, and it's about the only defeat the film received. It kicked the film industry's code right in the teeth, but it won the code's seal of approval and was shown on the nation's screens. It is still seen today on the television screen, and television has its own code prohibiting cruelty to animals.

Those who doubt that our affluent society is also an indifferent one need only look at the records: *Parents Magazine* gave the film its Special Merit Award, thus prompting humanitarians to suspect that the magazine had not a single parent on its editorial staff; the Film Estimate Board rated the picture as "Family Entertainment," but perhaps the board lacks a code; the Legion of Decency rated the film as A-I, or acceptable; and The Protestant Motion Picture Council concluded that "its more cruel and gory aspects are not emphasized," words that didn't solace or save the bulls who were slowly bled to death in the name of entertainment. Thus encouraged, it's a wonder the producer didn't follow up his success with *Ritual Slaughter*. Such a film might win a federal seal of approval. But a Special Merit Award will not be accepted as valid again by those who, under its influence, arranged showings of *The Brave One* for youth groups interested in animal welfare, humane education and conservation.

For reasons of economy, local color and authenticity, bullfight films are made abroad, but the most innocent of movie fans must know something about film production; that it's a rarity when a given scene is shot just once. Thus a given bull, already punched full of holes, must be patched up again and again until the desired film footage is just right. It can take days, and if the bull dies, another can be cut up in his place.

Other films employing animals are being made abroad with increasing frequency by American companies, none of them particularly interested in their own code, and all of them sure—since there are plenty of precedents—that the films will win approval for release here.

A film may not even need official approval. If it is made outside the United States, it may be considered not to require a code seal. Like the recently released picture *Sadismo,* which was made in Japan and featured, as a very small part of its offerings: baby chicks fed alive to a large lizard, a chained bear shot full of arrows by a group of children before being skinned alive, and a caged monkey whose head is shaved and split to provide a gourmet meal. The film was withdrawn after a storm of public protest.

State anticruelty laws, not the film code, prevent the filming of scenes of cruelty to animals in this country. But overseas, where dollars are welcome, a company can always find a place to film such entertaining scenes as jungle animals fighting to the death, or a hundred vicious dogs attacking a herd of a thousand horses, or the shooting of angry, starved, caged lions, or the piling-up of chariots thanks to good old Running W. Those are just a few of the mild scenes that grace the screens of our local theaters, and later—since old films never die—those with an appetite for cruelty can see them again on their television screens.

"The use of animals both in the production of television programs and as a part of television program content shall, at all times, be in conformity with accepted standards of humane treatment." That's the wording of the television code as worked out by The National Association of Broadcasters with representatives of the humane movement. Sixty percent of the commercial television stations in the United States, the three networks included, subscribe to the code. But some of the networks' affiliated stations do not subscribe to the code.

In general, then, the television industry does not have the code coverage that the film industry enjoys (but doesn't enforce). Four out of every ten television stations feel perfectly free to program material demonstrating cruelty to animals.

The films of yesteryear are shown again and again on television, and when it's a western, or a bullfight, or a *Ben-Hur,* or a jungle film, it's almost a sure bet that some of the animals involved were overworked, abused, and otherwise mistreated to achieve the desired entertaining effect. The exceptions are very few. The beloved nature films, supposedly shot without prior direction of the animals, are not so pure as the public has been led to believe. Wild animals do not, as a rule, cavort for the cameras on schedule. Each time such a film is televised, two codes are broken. Evidently, two wrongs make a right.

Nor are producers who make television film series using animals innocent of encouraging cruelty. It is not uncommon for a producer to buy film footage made by an independent cameraman, one who has staged animal fights unsupervised, using the old jungle film method. Two animals are tied with wire and brought in contact with each other; the wire keeps them from running away. The directors can thus goad them into fighting and when they stop goad them again. It is not uncommon to see animals thrown into scenes or off roofs as they supposedly arrive to join combat with man or animal.

Code or no code, an increasing number of stations are featuring bullfights as highlights of their programming. Not staged fights, but tapes of real fights, most of them taking place in Mexico. And all of the networks and most of the stations feature rodeo events from time to time. It is as if the television executives are unaware of the brutalities inflicted upon rodeo livestock and have never received letters of indignation from viewers.

Obviously, the television code doesn't apply to film produced by others, or to coverage of so-called sporting events promoted by others. Where, then, does it apply? To programs originated by television and thus the medium's entire responsibility? One would hope so, but there's no real evidence to support the hope, and ample evidence to prove that television is so far removed from its code that it has become a law unto itself. Consider this buffalo hunt scene, filmed exclusively for television:

The setting was a federal game refuge, a sanctuary for buffalo and other wild animals, all under the protective wing of the Federal Government. Since the script called for a buffalo to be killed, the director decided to resort to the Running W. The chosen buffalo was rigged with the device, men on horseback chased him, and down went the buffalo. The buffalo suffered internal injuries and died several days later. Meanwhile, television had defied its own code and, just for good measure, had broken both federal and state laws. The film has since been telecast by many of the stations that swear by the industry's code.

So, the television industry, although a late starter

in the entertainment field, is even with the film industry in not adhering to its own humane code. Unlike Hollywood, however, the young medium has been doing some soul searching, or listening to sponsors. The Television Code Review Board of the Code Authority of The National Association of Broadcasters has reviewed the subject of arena-originated bullfights and has reaffirmed existing code policy that such programs shown on subscriber (to the code) stations in their entirety are unacceptable under code standards. "In their entirety" are the key words, or loopholes, in this reaffirmation of a code that is generally disregarded anyway.

One might look for support, of course, to the sponsors. But the sponsors of such programs as bullfighting and rodeos feel no sense of responsibility: "Our participation in this program series involves only commercial presentations. Responsibility for the programming itself rests in the hands of the network and we do not have control over it. In this we are not given the opportunity to review programs in advance. Allowed this opportunity, we would have disassociated ourselves before the telecast. We agree with you; we don't think it was in the best interests of the general public." And this from the sponsor of one of the goriest bullfight films televised in recent years: "In my personal judgment, it is a display of cruelty, and I do not believe that cruelty can ever be used as a criterion for bravery. I have seen these exhibitions myself, and I do not personally approve of them."

If the sponsors are to be believed, they don't know what they're buying, and their products should be forgiven. Since television time is costly and sponsors do jockey for the best spots, the plea is hard to believe. A more honest one might be, "We do not have a code."

There's no simple explanation or cure for the paradox of big business: abhorring cruelty to animals on the one hand and promoting it with the other. If this is puzzling, consider the non-code television stations which shy away from bullfight programs and carry every rodeo program offered to them. Or consider one of the networks: "Whenever rodeos are scheduled to be presented over the ABC Television Network, we ascertain that the production of such program has been conducted under the supervision of the American Humane Association whose headquarters are in Denver, Colorado." No rodeo in history has ever been approved by a humane society and none ever will be, and ABC, if innocent of those facts, might reread its own code and concentrate on the noble words, "The use of animals shall at all times be in conformity with accepted standards of humane treatment."

A rodeo in which humane treatment was afforded the animals wouldn't be very popular, for it would lack the thrills induced by the bucking strap, the electric prods, and other such activators. And the sled wouldn't be there to drag away the dead calf, and the spectators would have no reason to hear the announcer's soothing words of "Don't worry, folks. The little fellow isn't hurt. Just had the wind knocked out of him."

Right down the line, big business continues to support big business when it comes to cruelty to animals, and codes are no more than statements of good intentions. If close to ten million spectators (1967) are willing to pay good money to attend rodeos and, in their innocence, grant approval to the abuse of animals, then television knows that more innocent millions will view rodeo programs at home, and the sponsors know it, too. The pity of it is that both are increasing the public's appetite for the rodeo and its attendant cruelties to animals. Fifty American universities now feature rodeos as annual events. More and more cities and towns are adopting the rodeo as a money-making tourist attraction. There are close to 550 such annual events right now, and the total prize money is pushing four million dollars. The Chamber of Commerce in Denver, Dallas, Cheyenne, Houston and Fort Worth find the rodeo a godsend, and in little Sydney, Iowa—not even a dot on most maps—rodeo week has kept civic programs solvent for over forty years. Here and there, as in Sydney, the American Legion is sponsor. Does anyone still wonder why anticruelty laws aren't pressed?

Everybody profits except the animals, and hardly anybody wants to listen to the truth. It's a generally dismal picture, and the only candles burning are in Ohio, New York, Connecticut, Rhode Island, West Virginia, Michigan, Illinois, California, Pennsylvania, Arkansas and Maryland. But efforts to ban the rodeo in all those states have failed, and future efforts may be just as disappointing. Not all of the people in all of the states are indifferent. Just most of them.

Man's Best Friend 12

OF ALL THE WORLD'S ANIMALS, WILD AND DOMESTIC, the dog is recognized as man's best friend. Cat fanciers argue this point, but not the cat. He doesn't quite trust man and remains a little independent, proving that he is smarter than the dog. It is as if the cat suspects that it's dangerous to be the best friend of man, and that he's better off as a mere acquaintance.

The cat is right. In general, he's not abused as much as the dog. While the cat and the dog share such man-inflicted cruelties as abandonment, animal farms and laboratories, there are some indignities that the average cat is spared. The blood lovers do not promote cat fights, for example, nor do the sports promote cat races.

Man's best friend for dog racing is the swift Greyhound, and since winters can be cold in the North, over half of the three dozen racetracks in this country are in Florida. Sooner or later, the best of the racing Greyhounds do their racing there, and the state's take in taxes runs to about twenty million dollars a year.

So dog racing is more big business than sport. This is reflected by the price tags: several thousand dollars for a winning adult, five hundred dollars and more for a pup whose breeding promises running potential. Not as expensive as a good fighting dog, perhaps, but the money is still an investment, and the racing dog's owner wants it returned with interest.

Most racing dog owners train their own dogs. The training starts at an early age, usually at about four months, and the objective is twofold: to develop running speed and to mold temperament. This makes the Greyhound an ideal student. The breed, one of the oldest on record, was originally developed for the chase. Its natural instinct is to hunt and, unlike other hound breeds, it depends more on sight than on nose. It's as if every Greyhound were born to chase a mechanical rabbit around a racetrack.

The racing pup's instinct for the chase is whetted by starting him on live rabbits. He has no trouble at all in outrunning the rabbit of the day, and his reward is the taste of fresh blood. Next the rabbit's speed is increased by attaching him to a mechanical lure that revolves in front of the dog to attract him to run in pursuit. The pup must run faster for his taste of blood, and he does. It can be argued that the only cruelty in the training is suffered by the rabbit, but that's not the case. Hand in hand with the pup's speed, his new personality is developed.

Down through the ages, or from around 2700 B.C., the Greyhound has been known for its lovable, tractable, gentle nature. Indeed, today's fanciers of the breed—aside from the sporting set—boast of its ideal disposition and its fondness for the company of children. So the breed's instinctive personality is an amenable one, or just what the racing dog's owner doesn't want. His ideal is a mean, hungry dog, one that will run his heart out to get to that rabbit, real or mechanical, and tear it to shreds.

Work on the pup when he's young enough and the personality of a pup of any breed can be changed. Beat him enough, deny him all affection, and underfeed him, and pretty soon the pup will become a mean, high-strung dog. So the racing dog matures into a hungry, always underweight dog, who dislikes people. And if his owner isn't careful he also dislikes other dogs. The risk of dog-fights during a race is lessened by a couple of golden training rules: pups grow up together and adults work together. So the racers are accustomed to the company of other dogs.

The only inconvenience for the owner-trainer is the fact that Florida and the other host states for dog racing all frown upon the practice of using live rabbits, or live anything else, as training lures. So a great deal of the early training is done in the plains states, where remote areas are still available and small wild game is abundant. Those states frown also, but law enforcement is difficult in the wide, open spaces. If there have been any arrests, they haven't been recorded.

The average owner-trainer considers himself an honest and compassionate man. Honest, because dog racing is honest—after all, the dog is running strictly on his own and has no jockey aboard him. And compassionate, because he doesn't really expect his dogs to win every time out. All he asks of his dogs is that they win often enough to meet expenses and raise his own standard of living.

It's true that dog racing is honest, or as honest as any form of racing can be. It's carefully supervised, and the tricks of the trade to keep a dog from winning are more difficult to get away with these days: emery-rubbed, sensitive foot pads, toenails too short, pads tied together, and drugs. And perhaps the owners are compassionate in their ways. After all, the racing dog who cannot win has no future at the tracks and, since he's vicious, no future as a pet. All of the racing Greyhounds can't be consistent winners, and the majority can't win often enough to cover the expenses of their keep. Most are dead weights, money-eaters, losers.

Every year, hundreds of losers disappear from the tracks. Where do they go? What happens to them? Humane society agents in Florida figure that only about a thousand a year are killed in that state. What happens to all the other losers? We can only suspect; we'll never know.

The racing dog, of course, is just one of man's best friends. Another is the show dog, and in this country he can be a Greyhound or one of 115 other breeds and varieties recognized by the American Kennel Club. In a sense, the show dog is the aristocrat of dogdom, for he is or should be the epitome of his breed. This is not always the case, of course, for at any one of the hundreds of annual dog shows one may see dreadful specimens of many breeds. The dogs don't know this and their owners won't believe it. Pride in one's dog is akin to pride in one's self.

Nobody denies the worthy intent behind dog shows. They started long before dogs became big business. They began as rather social gatherings and were attended mostly by breeders interested in seeing how their dogs compared with those of others. It was pleasant to win, of course, but more important to learn something of value and then go home and apply it in one's breeding program. Improvement of the breeds was the main, overall objective. That's not the way it is today. Winning is important, and somehow the show dog's glory reflects upon the owner, although only the owner seems to be aware of it. And dog shows, all sponsored by local kennel clubs, have become money machines for just about everybody but the sponsors, the breeders and the owners. The money spills into the bank accounts of professional handlers, kennel managers, judges, importers and show superintendents. Only the dogs suffer. Not all of them, but enough of them.

It's a strange life for the show Poodle. His coat is all-important, and a little arsenic is added to his daily diet to keep it in bloom. To keep every hair in that coat from damage, he must lead a life of restricted movement. He spends it alone, perched on a shelf or in a tiny pen, except when nature calls—and then he exercises alone. And, of course, his tail must be docked.

The Boxer, another breed with docked tail, undergoes ear cropping at an early age. Even when the pup's ears are cut under anesthetic, the aftereffects and the long healing period are painful. If the ears are ever going to stand properly, they must heal first from the inside, or just the opposite of nature's own inclination. Thus the outer portions must be kept open and raw for several weeks. Every day, the natural scabs must be "cracked" and the pup screams his agony. There's never been any justification for this cruelty, except that lovers of the Boxer want his ears to stand erect. The breed's official standard, written by humans and approved all these years by the American Kennel Club, insists on the cropped ears. The same can be said for several other breeds. It's strange that the American Kennel Club continues to sanction this abuse, and stranger still that so many prominent Americans have never raised the slightest objection. Prominent? The horse-show world, so proud of its roster of owners, must take a back seat when it comes to the show dog fancy, for its list of great names is just as wealthy and socially prominent, and much, much longer.

Strangest of all, perhaps, is the fact that several enlightened states now have laws calling the cropping of dog's ears cruel and unlawful (with fines up to $250), and nothing is done to enforce such laws. In those very states, numerous dog shows are held every year and the cropped dogs are shown; breeders in those states continue to crop ears, and often botch the job, so that the dogs can never be shown; and veterinarians, licensed by the states, continue to crop ears for a fee.

Why do veterinarians, of all people, continue to

cooperate? Business is business, perhaps. Certainly no one can say with certainty that the process improves a dog's appearance. Even if the "expert" manages not to botch the job, as so many do, the cropping that looked good on the puppy may not fit the proportions of the mature dog. Furthermore, the operation itself contains risks, and the pain and discomfort of the healing period may permanently damage a pup's disposition.

Various members of the vet profession have published articles on the dog's tail, however, and have reached the conclusion that nature put the tail there to improve the dog's balance, help his circulatory system and encourage his dietary processes. Others have reasoned that the docking of a dog's tail, since it defies nature's intent, induces early heart trouble.

Still, veterinarians go right on docking tails, and the American Kennel Club, dedicated as it is to the improvement of all their recognized breeds, feels that cropping, or docking, or both tend to improve the Boxer, Poodle, Kerry Blue Terrier, German Short-haired Pointer, and most of the spaniels and terriers, but that it would be terrible to go against nature and do the same to the setters, retrievers, and the majority of the other breeds.

Away from racing and the shows, man's most popular best friend is the hunting dog. Humanitarians and conservationists are in his debt, for additional millions of wild creatures and birds would suffer lingering, painful deaths if he weren't around to find and retrieve the wounded for the men with guns. But the trained hunting dog leads a life of confusion. He's supposed to flush the boar, but not attack it—unless the game warden is absent, and then he should attack. He's supposed to chase deer during the open season, but not the closed, when —if observed—somebody is likely to shoot him. He's trained to flush birds and retrieve them, but must disregard them one day when he's on a private journey and he chances upon a yardful of chickens.

Of all the breeds, the hunters—hounds and sporting dogs—get into the most trouble if allowed to run loose. They are also the most likely to be kidnapped, and not necessarily for the laboratories. Most of our thirty million hunters don't own dogs, but wish that they did, and are not above stealing. In almost every state, thousands of Beagles disappear just before the rabbit season opens.

The owner's alternative is to keep his hunting dog confined when not hunting. So many a hunting dog lives most of his life locked up in a kennel run at a gun club, a boarding kennel, or at home. From that confinement, on the day of the hunt, many a dog travels in the trunk of a car and some die along the way. Suffocation and carbon monoxide poisoning are fatal for dogs as well as humans. It's a common occurrence, as common as being shot to death after the hunting season. Who wants to feed a stolen dog for the next ten months, or until another open season rolls around? Too expensive, and so easy to steal another one next year. In comparison, those who abandon dogs seem like humanitarians.

Insofar as hounds are concerned, this end-of-the-season carnage seems to be lightest in our southern states. That's where coon-on-the-log contests are held the year 'round, and hounds—purebred or mixed—make ideal participants. In the contest, a raccoon is chained to a log, which is set afloat on a pond. The rules call for the dog to topple the raccoon into the water. Dog after dog is sent out from the bank, and the winning dog is the one who topples the raccoon in the shortest elapsed time. After the winner has been declared and all bets are paid, there's a grand climax—if the raccoon is still alive. All the dogs are sent out in a body to finish him off. In Georgia, lovers of this grand climax still talk about the time forty dogs, each averaging over fifty pounds, went out to get a weary, twenty-pound raccoon. Five dogs drowned before the other thirty-five made mincemeat of the raccoon.

There's a slight variation on this contest called coon-in-a-hole. In this the raccoon is chained in a hole, and the dogs are sent after him en masse. The winner is the dog that pulls the raccoon out of the hole. To win, he often has to fight off other dogs. It's a popular pastime in Texas, and the winning dog often takes a worse beating than the raccoon. Usually, at least one dog loses an eye. If the raccoon survives, he's pushed back into the hole to await yet another gang of dogs.

Years ago, these contests were witnessed by men only. Men still dominate the spectator ranks, but now the sponsors permit family nights, when a man can bring along his wife and children. This shocked the Dallas Federation of Women's Clubs (15,000 members) and it urged the Texas legislature to pass laws banning the contests. Nothing happened. And in Tuscaloosa, Alabama, the Ministerial Association found the contests "inhumane, cruel, brutal and ruthless," and then resolved to condemn such "animal torture, cruelty and suffering." Perhaps taking its cue from Texas, the Association did not call upon a law from the Alabama legislature. In both states, existing anticruelty laws make the contests unlawful, but there hasn't been any curtailing of the contests. Those who hold public office prefer not to offend the voters, and many of the South's finest citizens were weaned on coon contests.

Man's best friend is most populous, of course, as the pet dog. Since he and the pet cat number about forty million each, and well over a hundred million puppies and kittens are born each year (better than 10,000 every hour), there's always a surplus. This surplus would be even greater and the country would be in danger of pet dog and cat dictatorship if it were not for the fact that the majority of puppies and kittens are unwanted. An easy sixty million babies a year are drowned, shot, banged over the head, abandoned, buried alive or tossed into garbage cans. This wholesale murder happens at every social level and is the net result of stupidity and carelessness on the part of owners. A college education and parenthood itself do not prepare some people for the certainty that a bitch in season or a female cat in estrus is going to get herself bred, come hell or high water, if given the chance. Tens of thousands of people, bank presidents and mothers of seven among them, tie bitches in heat to a rope in the backyard, never look out the window, and then wonder how on earth their pets became pregnant. This carelessness is repeated the next time the bitch is in heat. Some people never learn, or don't want to learn, or believe that bitches in heat are disobedient and can't be trusted.

It's true that thousands of owners of unwanted pups do have a conscience and are not cold-blooded. They are the ones who make a sincere effort to place the pups in homes, usually as gifts. But something free is rarely as valued as something purchased. Gift pups often get a minimum of attention, and some new owners—since they have not a penny of investment in the pets—do not visit a veterinarian when the need is obvious. Let the pup die, and if another one is wanted, there's always somebody around willing to replace him.

The pet-dog surplus is not restricted to canines of doubtful lineage. Some four million purebred pups are born every year, and in many breeds the supply amounts to more than the demand. Department stores, mail-order houses, puppy farms and pet shops offer the purebred surplus at bargain prices, often below what a serious breeder would spend to bring pups to a saleable age. The bargain, purebred pups are seldom of quality, but the market for them seems to be there. So much so, in fact, that some puppy farms now specialize in importing litters from England and offering them at bargain prices. This helps the surplus problem in England, but it adds to the dilemma here. The bargain pup is only slightly better off than the free pup, and the female usually costs less than the male. The retailers have no trouble moving the bitches, usually the most difficult sex to give away.

The free pups, the bargain purebreds, and the five-dollar mongrels would, if granted the right, rename Labor Day as Abandonment Day. All over America, this day spells the end of summer vacation, and all over America the summer visitors close their cottages and return to the cities. Hundreds of thousands of them abandon their dogs. They can't keep dogs in the city, or they just wanted playmates for the kids anyway. Dogs aren't the only pets abandoned in this heartless fashion, but they are in the majority. Some end up in dog pounds, some in humane shelters, and a few find new homes on their own. More starve to death, and even more are killed on the highways. Some are poisoned, some are shot, and an amazing number manage to survive on their own until they meet a pack of wild dogs.

Our feral dog population amounts to about fifteen million. Abandoned dogs, lost dogs, neglected dogs and plain bad dogs add to the wild pack population every year. The homeless dogs roam all over America, usually within range of human habitation, and sometimes they invade the hearts of cities. For the most part, they are mongrels, and some can trace their ancestry back to before the white man came to America. The Indians had dogs, and some of them turned wild.

Today, packs average from a few dogs to a few dozen. Most are mongrels, but purebreds, former pets, run with them, and Collies, German Shepherd Dogs, Doberman

Pinschers and even Beagles are sighted frequently. They breed, of course, but the very nature of their life—always on the move and hunting for food—is against successful litter raising. Wild game, livestock, and sometimes human beings are their targets, and they are a constant rabies threat. In Virginia, game wardens shoot better than forty thousand a year. This prevents dogs from killing deer, a right reserved for hunters, poisoners, trappers, farmers, gardeners and drivers. But despite shooting and poisoning campaigns in many states, the feral dog population continues to explode. Not because of their own breeding success, but because so many of our citizens do not regard abandonment or neglect a sin, or proper care a virtue. So we even have a wild canine surplus.

Man's best friend, when he's wild, is the only dog as smart as the cat. He's found a way to be independent, and to survive without man.

And what about feral cats? There are millions of them, too, but they don't travel in packs, and there's never been a reasonable estimate of their total number. In any event, it's a shifting population. The pet cat can adjust swiftly to the wild and then, after weeks or months, return home and readjust at once to domestic status. But in all areas of the country, wherever the human population increases, the feral cat population also increases. A fair indication that cat owners are just as careless as dog owners.

Fortunately, there's a remedy for the surplus pet problem, and it amounts to a pet-owner education program. If the owners who don't want their bitches or lady cats to breed would spay the bitches and neuter the cats, then the millions of unwanted puppies and kittens would never be born. It's a simple, painless, inexpensive operation, and doesn't damage the patient's health in the least.

One sure way of curbing the mass production of unwanted pups and kittens would be to charge an excessive license fee, twenty-five to fifty dollars, for unspayed bitches and unneutered lady cats. The plan isn't new and the humane movement has been pushing it for a long time. To be at all effective, it would have to be enforced by state law and veterinarians would be required to perform the simple operation for a minimum fee. But politicians would rather not offend pet-owning voters, and veterinary associations have not been eager to establish minimum fees. Therefore, America can look forward to an ever-increasing population of unwanted dogs and cats.

Anyone doubting the need for such a plan can have that doubt dispelled by a little mathematics. If a given bitch produces an evenly divided litter of four pups—two males, two females—and the females live and whelp evenly divided litters of pups, and this process continues in the same manner through seven generations, then the grand total will be 4,372 pups, half of them female. If the original bitch is permitted complete freedom and allowed to breed twice a year, or each time she comes into season, then the seven-year (14-generation) total will be 9,540,912 pups. Cats usually enjoy—if that's the word—three estrous periods a year, and the first can come as early as five months of age. Thus, using the same formula of four evenly divided offspring per litter, a given queen can be responsible for a seven-year total that staggers the imagination. And a pregnant cat can go right back into estrus and breed again and carry two litters of different ages at the same time! And go right on doing this into her twentieth year!

The people who are worrying about a takeover from outer space might devote a little of that time to better purpose by worrying about the cat takeover.

The Forgotten 13

THERE ARE SOME MILLION AND A HALF TO TWO MILlion feral swine in the United States. They outnumber all other feral livestock combined—horses, burros, cattle, sheep and goats. The swine take to the wild with great enthusiasm, and this may be proof of their high intelligence. Of all our livestock, we are deepest in debt to the pig, yet we give him the rawest deal. So, in nineteen of our states, including Hawaii, he no longer wants anything to do with man. Feral swine are listed as game animals in a few states and protected in none. Gaunt, lean, long-legged, long-snouted animals, they don't look much like the typical pig, and their meat isn't prized by gourmets.

The pig was domesticated for man's table. It has always been his main purpose in life, except for a period of time in ancient Egypt when he was revered as a deity. It wasn't a unique honor, for the Egyptians revered other animals, too, but for a while pigs lived long enough to die natural deaths, and that was unique.

All other pigs are born to be slaughtered. Today the pig contributes 75 pounds of pork and 15 pounds of lard to the average American's diet yearly, plus indeterminate amounts of sausage, hocks, ham, cutlets, and chitling. He also supplies belts, gloves, billfolds and handbags, as well as insulin and a list of pharmacopoeia that includes cortisone, ACTH, epinephrine, liver extract, bile salts, thyroid extract and many others. And the suture material used by surgeons comes from the pig. There's an old saying around packing houses to the effect that man uses all of the pig except the squeal.

Pound for pound, he must be judged our most valuable member of the livestock family. There are those who rate him behind the cow in importance, but he's cheaper to raise because he converts grain into meat much more efficiently. A fattening pig will turn 425 pounds of grain into 100 pounds of personal weight, almost all of it usable. To gain the same weight, a steer requires 1,000 pounds of grain and hay, and a lamb 900. But a pig doesn't need grain to pack on the weight. He will accept and convert almost any sort of foodstuff into weight, and that's the reason why so many garbage collectors have always raised swine and the public has conceived of the pig as a smelly animal. Raised in clean surroundings, the pig will thrive and prove to be the least odorous of our large farm animals.

In the lifetime of the American pig, his one consolation is that he won't be subjected to ritual slaughter. More often than not, this is no consolation at all, for the average slaughterhouse still does things in the old way: shackle, hoist, poleax, throat-slit, and then the dip into the vat; the pig, sometimes conscious, still alive.

Things are usually worse back on the farm. The pigs not destined for the marketplace are raised for the farmer's own larder. There's nothing wrong with that form of economy, and more pigs are slaughtered at home than any of our other large meat animals. The wrong lies in the manner of the slaughter. The farmer or economy-minded owner may be a college graduate, but he doesn't change the old family tradition on hog-killing day.

For those who have never witnessed this scene, here is an extract from a letter to the editor of *The Voice of the Voiceless:*

> As a child on the farm I found the pig to be an animal with much affection and intelligence when treated as one of God's creatures. They would respond to love and kindness with almost as much affection as the dog to its keeper.
>
> Hog killing times are still hateful memories to my mind. I still remember a big frosty morning during late October, spoken of as hog killing weather. The fires were lit, the water put on the heat, the knives sharpened and the small arms brought out, while the helpless ones waited for their death. Would the blow from the ax be quick with death? If the pistol was used, would the executioner find the mark? Would the knife find its way? If so, the victims would find an easy death. But if there was a slip of the eye or hand the cry of the tortured in its lingering death would vibrate across the hills like souls of the damned.
>
> Even today I can hear the squealing of the hogs in their death agonies, the laughter of the men, the justification for the miss of ax, gun, or knife. Yes, the killing of these creatures was a morning of fun, pleasure and big eating for the unfeeling men and women who failed to teach their children mercy and pity.
>
> Too often the child's "education" obtained at hog killing has been one of the driving forces in manhood. This force has been so strong that it has driven

its victims to murder of human beings. Much of this comes from lessons learned in the killing of farm animals.

Things haven't changed on the farm, except that the sledgehammer is now considered a handier and less messy executioner's weapon than the ax. Hammer or ax, the method must be considered slighter one barbaric degree than the old-fashioned method used on about half the farms. This calls for jabbing a knife into the pig's jugular vein and letting him bleed to death. The theory is that the slow, agonizing death keeps the meat from spoiling, although such is not the case. Millions of pigs die this way every year on farms and in old-fashioned slaughterhouses. Still, this final brutality is in keeping with the way the pig is treated all during his brief life on hog farms large and small. Young boars undergo castration in the fashion of young bulls on the range: without anesthetic and given nothing to relieve the after-pain. Instead of branding, the pigs undergo notching, or a series of identifying cuts in the sensitive flesh of the ears. And then there is the little matter of ringing, in which an iron ring is driven through the flesh between the nostrils to keep the pigs from their favorite pastime of rooting in the fields. Inexpert hands often handle the castrating, notching and ringing, but even in expert hands the practices bring the severest of pains to the pigs. For miles around a hog farm, all the neighbors know when it's one of those painful days. The symphony of agonized shrieks is deafening.

Now man has developed a breed of pig not destined

for the nation's tables. He's known as the minipig and at maturity weighs no more than forty pounds. He was developed for the research laboratories, and scientists feel that he'll be a better subject than the dog and cat for the study of certain diseases. That sounds reasonable. Man and pig digestive systems and skins are quite similar, and there are other close physiological relationships. The minipig will be easy to operate upon, cheap to feed, and best of all—from a laboratory's viewpoint—a means to take the heat off the mounting pressures from critics. The sensibilities of the millions of cat and dog lovers are touched when they learn about the treatment their favorites receive in the laboratories, but few people care about what happens to pigs.

So once again, and in an entirely new way, the pig will be serving mankind and increasing our knowledge. There's no way of guaranteeing that he won't suffer as much as the laboratory cats and dogs, but at least he won't have to experience the mistreatment of the animal dealer farms. Not for a while anyway. How does one steal a minipig?

Overall, the only real progress made in the pig's behalf can be credited to the George A. Hormel Company of Minnesota, where a method of anesthetizing hogs before slaughter was developed. Thus some much needed humaneness has been introduced by one major packer, and a few others have since followed suit. The rest of the meat industry stands pat, unimpressed and unwilling to absorb the small, additional cost of compassion.

While a few pigs do find relief at trail's end, the

same claim can't be made for that other favorite of the nation's appetite, the chicken. This lesser, winged creature has fewer defenders than the pig, although he goes to the marketplace at the rate of five billion a year, or better than three times the total of all meat animals combined. Translate that into chicken soup (two percent chicken, by law) and discover a new ocean.

The chicken does have intelligence, although the degree is debatable, and he does suffer pain as acutely as any warm-blooded animal. He is always conscious at the moment of slaughter. A knife is stuck through his mouth and into his brain. Then the knife is drawn across an artery in the interior of the throat. Not a humane method, for the pain is intense and the knife doesn't always pierce the brain. Executed properly, it does have the virtue of limited pain duration—as compared to the bleeding of the pig.

A quick death, if it happens that way, is about the only break a chicken gets these days. The poultry business is big, organized and efficient. The incubators in an average, commercial hatchery turn out better than three million chicks a year, and all of the healthy ones start living the life of machines. Packed into cardboard cartons when they're only hours old, the females are shipped off to the egg farms and the males to the broiler plants. Ten thousand chicks, packed a hundred per carton, constitute a not unusual shipment. They need warmth, and they get it from the combined heat of their own tiny bodies. They don't require food or water for forty-eight hours.

Brooder houses await them at their new home, they find food for the first time, and the regimented life begins. Instinct guides them to food and water. As they move around in close quarters, they shove, peck and trample each other. There are always fatalities, although the losses are less severe at modern poultry plants where heating, food, and a program of immunization against fowl diseases are scientifically planned. But whether the plant is up-to-date or not, the big problem is overcrowding. The temptation to house a thousand growing birds where only five hundred belong is great, and overcrowding is an open invitation to cannibalism. More fatalities result.

When they're old enough—anywhere from three to six months, depending on the breed—the surviving pullets are moved into the laying house. They spend the rest of their lives there, two years at best, or as long as they can produce a sufficient number of eggs. The dropouts, or culls, are the ones who don't produce, and they become the fryers in the marketplace.

The building known as a laying house is old-fashioned and the term is something of a misnomer these days, for the modern egg plant confines pullets and hens in battery cages. Each bird occupies her own cramped apartment, with 81 square inches of floor space customary for a Leghorn, and slightly larger cages for the bigger breeds. The cages are piled row on row and give the laying house the look of a prison. After standing on the mesh floors of these wire cages for a period of time, hens lose the use of their legs. Under normal conditions, exercise is important to a hen's ability to lay: her natural movements aid the egg in its downward progress. Now man has substituted high-powered food supplements and continuous lights for nature's slower, less productive methods. Continuous lights lengthen the laying hen's day. The egg plants put the lights on early and turn them off late to give every hen the maximum opportunity to produce. Billions of caged hens think that the night is four hours long.

Whether the long working day and the small prison cells constitute cruelties or not seems to be a matter of personal opinion. Poultry men don't think they're being cruel to the hens ("The best-kept chickens in the world"), and nobody has come along to prove that the hens undergo any physical or psychological suffering. Still, the extra-long day and the battery cage are not a chicken's birthrights, and the innovations haven't improved hen habits. The best ones still lay but one egg per day, and the size of that egg is still the same. And in the end the old hen becomes a roaster that is no tenderer than the one that knew a more natural life.

That's the story of the female chick, from hatch to death. The male chick starts out the same way, but he's hardly old enough to know that he's a cockerel when the killing knife turns him into a broiler. He's eight to twelve weeks old when killing day comes, and the precise span of his short life is determined by rate of growth and market conditions. Before that final, searing pain, a selected number of the young ones may have survived the caponizing knife—and been shown as little consideration as are the young bulls when castrated. The minority who become capons live another seven or eight months until they're big and plump and their flesh is tender. Then it's doomsday for them.

It's on the small poultry farms—and there are more small ones than big ones—that the overcrowding of chickens takes place and the fatality percentage runs high. Most of these farms run from a few hundred to two thousand birds, and they are part-time or supplemental income operations. Cannibalism is often avoided by a simple operation known as debeaking. This is painful and it makes dining difficult, but chickens are stubborn and refuse to starve. And aside from cannibalism, overcrowding means such threats as disease and trampling, plus the even bigger danger of heat. The chicken has no sweat glands to assist in keeping the body cool, and a ninety-degree day means that chickens are dying.

The only law devised by man to protect the chicken is a local one. It prohibits the sale of baby chicks, in natural or dyed colors, by pet stores and department stores and other retail outlets. These are the Easter season chicks, bought as gifts for children and literally loved to death by them. The law has been adopted in many communities, and is enforced in some. It's a great law, and all it needs is public support. If a doting mother wishes to give a lavender chick to each child at her son's birthday party, she'll find the chicks somewhere. If the chief of police wants a polka-dot chick for his grandson, he'll find it somewhere. Whatever the colors, ninety-nine percent of the gift chicks will be dead within days.

Just about the only view the public gets of poultry mistreatment, and not too many regard it as such, is the common one of a crate-laden truck careening down the highway. The crates are piled ten high, and every crate is overpopulated with live chickens. Just a joyride to a non-happy ending, and some of the winged passengers will be dead upon arrival. Is their destination a live poultry market or a slaughterhouse plant? Or direct to a medical research laboratory?

Yes, chickens, and geese and ducks and other fowl, are as popular as the furry creatures in the research laboratories and are equally mistreated. The mature birds help our scientists in their quest for new knowledge. And the young ones, the chicks, are helping our boys and girls in their review of old knowledge on the dissecting tables of biology classes all over the land. They are even earning fame for budding teen-age scientists at the school science fairs: needle-inject the right formula into incubating eggs, and deformed chicks will hatch. When the chicks die, stick each one into a glass jar of preservative and exhibit the jars at the science fair. It's a sure winner in the Home Project Class.

And then there's the case of the rabbit. He's one of our more abundant creatures, and his issue is even more popular than baby chicks at Easter time. At the tender age of four to six weeks, the bunny goes into hundreds of thousands of homes and apartments, and many don't last very long. Those that do are seldom retained as pets. Parents find it difficult to believe that a rabbit is as easy to housebreak as a dog, so the young ones who survive a couple of months are given their freedom in a patch of woods. The innocent bunny knows no fear. If he doesn't hop onto a highway and get flattened by a car, a stray cat will find him. The strays are always hungry.

The wild rabbit, of course, is big game to every small boy with a rifle, and few boys start out as crack shots. For every rabbit the boy kills, five or six more are wounded, and for them it's the old story of slow death in hiding.

The rabbit is also a favorite of the research laboratories, and millions are mistreated and die in those halls of science each year. Elsewhere, he's hunted, trapped, poisoned, skinned and butchered for his meat or pelt. None go to their deaths in humane ways. Perhaps those killed for their pelts would derive satisfaction from knowing that thousands of women who take pride in their "seal" or "beaver" or "ermine" coats are really wearing rabbit.

For almost a decade now, the little town of Harmony, North Carolina, has made the rabbit a rather odd symbol of Christmas. The local post of the American Legion sponsors a charity banquet during the yuletide season, and rabbit is the chief item on the menu. To procure a sufficient supply of rabbits, hundreds of able-bodied citizens and youngsters fan out through the countryside and drive the frightened wild rabbits into fenced enclosures. When enough rabbits have been assembled in this manner, they are beaten to death by club-wielding and stone-throwing men, women and children, although adults with quick hands are able to catch rabbits, hold them by the rear legs, and bang them against the ground until dead.

North Carolina has its anticruelty laws, of course, but apparently they are suspended at Christmastime. When protests were made to the National Commander of the Legion, he bucked the matter through channels to the state Legion headquarters, and there the matter still rests.

If few people worry about the plight of the chicken and the rabbit, fewer still give any thought at all to the seal and our other marine mammals. This could be because seal meat has never been popular with us, or because—in a commercial sense—he is no longer any of our business. The seal and sea lion and sea otter are now protected in our coastal waters. In numbers, they don't amount to much anymore, so our own fur industry leaves them alone. On the other hand, the fishing industry thinks that the remaining sea lions eat too many salmon.

In recent years both the big Steller's sea lion and the California sea lion have reappeared and been thriving in that state's protected waters. Together, they amount to no more than 25,000, compared to millions before the turn of the century. But even before the total reached 25,000, the state senate, under pressure from the game department and commercial fishermen, passed a bill authorizing slaughter of seventy-five percent of the sea lions. Thanks to a huge public outcry, the bill didn't become law. Very little of a marine mammal's diet consists of salmon or other commercial fish. Indeed, one of his favorite dishes is the lamprey, the enemy of fish.

So the sea lions were not needlessly and foolishly slaughtered, and are in no danger of extinction at this time. But all the furor interested the fur industry, which was pleased to hear that the sea otter was back home again. This otter carries one of the world's most valuable furs on his back. He was so close to extinction fifty years ago that—by international treaty—he has been granted safety in most waters ever since. There are probably 2,000 of them off California's coast today, and there's hardly a fur industry executive in the country who doesn't dream of getting his hands on all of them.

Nobody is making a move to grab the protected seals. One very good reason is that North American waters not under jurisdiction of the United States still contain big numbers of unprotected seals. Of these the harp and hooded seals are the popular species in the seal hunts, and the chief hunters are from England and other European countries. The foreign firms hunt with a vengeance, slaughtering both young and old, and it won't be long before these seals are on the verge of extinction. With their fat, skins and fur, both seal pups and adults contribute to the economy of foreign lands. The annual seal toll is all out of proportion to the total seal population and breeding habits. England, the Netherlands, Norway, and other countries harvesting North American waters are hunting with the abandon of the Russians around Alaska a hundred years ago. The Newfoundland area, down to three million seals in 1950, is down to under one million now. In just two areas—one the Gulf of St. Lawrence—the 1966 toll was close to 300,000 baby seals alone. And, since methods haven't changed in the sealing industry, chances are that many of those babies were still alive when skinned.

If there's to be any future at all for seals, some must be allowed to breed, but the hunters have no regard for tomorrow and, apparently, their own business future. Seals are netted on their annual migration to the breeding grounds. The netted ones are kept under water for hours, until they drown. Other adults are shot in the water, and the wounded escape to die elsewhere. Breeding-age females are not spared, and the white, soft pelts of the baby hooded seals are much in demand.

The biggest hauls are made by gaffing and clubbing, usually done while the animals are on land. Dead or alive, the seals are dragged to the skinning area, and out come the knives. A kick between the eyes usually suffices for a pup. It doesn't always kill him, but his screams don't bother the skinner. It's all a part of the day's work to the man.

Although the slaughter takes place on our continent, and surely its methods are barbaric, the United States and Canada are powerless and can do nothing about it. Conservation is not a word that appeals to the seal hunters. They define it as saving a species from extinction by one group of humans so that another group can massacre it. It's a negative point of view, but it has its precedents.

The World Federation for the Protection of Animals, the Survival Service Commission of the International Union for the Conservation of Nature, and the International Commission for the Northwest Atlantic Fisheries are among the groups that could do something about the seal's plight, but they haven't. For years now, there's been talk that the United Nations might come to the rescue. Humane education is already a part of the UNESCO program, and a humane clause dropped into the Law of the Sea Conference could cover both the seal and the rapidly disappearing whale. But new human problems pop up with such frequency that the United Nations may never have the time to consider the ordeal of the sea mammals. And for many women, there's nothing quite as warm and dry as sealskin boots.

Time, it seems, is not on the side of the seals.

America the Beautiful 14

THE BILLBOARDS THAT CLUTTER OUR HIGHWAYS AND BLOT out the scenery have been under attack for a long time. They do not contribute to a beautiful America. Everyone, including the tenants of the White House, seems to agree on that point. If one percent of the effort devoted to the anti-billboard campaign were expended on the cleaning up of the roadside zoo mess, a great many animals would discover some beauty in America.

The roadside zoo is a peculiar sort of business enterprise based on the double premise that children love animals, or at least are fond of seeing animals, and that children give orders to their parents. The business flourishes wherever there is a tourist season, and is seldom an entity in itself. It is usually operated as the lure for stopovers at gas stations, dining spots, motels, picnic grounds, commercial parks, souvenir shops, camping grounds and other small businesses that dot our highways and help make America beautiful.

If the average zoo has a single virtue, it is that it is smaller than the average animal dealer's farm. Conditions are just as bad, but fewer animals are in custody. And if the zoos have any claim to fame, it is that local humane societies receive more complaints about them than any other form of animal abuse. Even tourists who love the bullfights in Spain are offended by the conditions and the smells of the roadside zoos.

The zoos take many forms, and none resembles a child's conception or remembrance of a legitimate zoo. These roadside versions, sometimes billed as educational exhibits, house their animals in a collection of cages, shacks, boxes, pits, wire pens and (for snakes) glass-covered counters. "Animals confined in small, dirty cages, all exposed and shelters inadequate," reads a humane agent's report. "Several animals suffering from disease, many without water. Veterinarian stated all animals in filthy condition and reported food both putrid and inedible. Exhibits included a 350-pound Himalayan bear, golden eagle, silver fox, Australian dingo, lion cub, two bear cubs, Japanese deer, African sheep, cranes, monkeys, red fox, a coati mundi and a porcupine." The report is typical, and so is the roadside zoo, which is still in operation. The only changes in the exhibits occur when animals die, and are replaced by living ones.

Bears and deer are the feature attractions at most roadside zoos, and in most states it is illegal to keep either of the animals in captivity. To do so, a special permit is required, and this is granted only for "educational or scientific purposes." But, oddly, the special permit does not require even minimum standards of housing and care. And more oddly still—since it is the state conservation department that issues the permit—the applicant's qualifications are not investigated, nor are his grounds inspected. The fee is never more than a few dollars, is renewed annually, and all transactions are handled by mail. Thus it's possible to own a roadside zoo full of bears, never feed them, and call the whole operation an educational exhibit.

The education provided never includes lectures or informative literature about the animals. It does provide an illustration of the way animals should not be treated, a point that somehow escapes the average tourist. He stops because he is curious about the animals, perhaps, or he may even be an animal lover. That would put him one up on the owner, who loves his animals in terms of dollars, and who knows even less than the tourist about proper care.

If he has one, the businessman's permit does not guarantee him freedom from state inspection. But this doesn't worry him. If an abundance of complaints is received, state inspectors will check on the zoo in question. The authorities arrive and ascertain that the owner does possess a special permit. Next, the animals are reviewed—but only those animals on the state's "protected list," such as deer and bear. The owner may receive a scolding and some sound advice, but that's all he has to worry about. No matter how deplorable the conditions at the zoo, the conservation departments are not empowered to invoke anticruelty laws, and therefore a man who owns a roadside zoo can get away with almost anything.

Many zoo owners do not feed their bears or other animals during the tourist season. They depend on the general public to feed the caged and penned animals, and they'll even provide the food to the public at a price. It may not be the right food for the animal, but that's unimportant, as long as the overhead is kept down and there's a profit in the till. When the bear wastes away on his diet of improper food, chewing gum, cigarette butts and buttons, it doesn't cost much to buy another one. A cub, usually—one sold to an animal dealer when his mother was shot illegally. Fawns are acquired in the same way. And no state licenses the animal dealers. They don't even need a permit.

When the tourist season ends, the roadside zoo goes into hibernation. The sign comes down, the gates are closed, and now the animals represent overhead and not profit. Sometimes they are removed to new quarters in an old barn or shed where they are expected to survive the winter months on insufficient diets of stale bread and garbage scraps. Heat is costly, so it is not provided. The exotic creatures from tropical lands face certain death.

Or, if providing food and shelter is too much trouble, the zoo keeper might unload his stock at the nearest animal farm. From there, the animal's road may lead to another roadside zoo, a research laboratory or a mail-order house. The raccoon or monkey anyone can buy through the mails is often a roadside zoo veteran and a poor bet for a long, healthy life.

Why do the roadside zoos continue to flourish, why are there more of them every year, and why doesn't somebody do something about them? Why aren't there licenses and regulations and supervision? Where are the progressive conservation departments, the wildlife agencies, the alert health authorities? And where are all those men in uniform who are supposed to be enforcing the anticruelty laws?

Only the humane societies appear to be waging a war on the roadside zoos, and their record of success is a skimpy one. It is as if the zoos were medical laboratories and benefiting man and therefore worthy of immunity. Even in New York State, where humanitarians pursue cruelty to animals with a vengeance, the roadside zoo manages somehow to escape all penalty. In one recent case that must have shocked all who read about it, charges against three owners of a game park (New York has much fancier names for roadside zoos) were dismissed because the local judge found that they were not responsible for their collection of dehydrated, starving, or starved-to-death wild animals. Nor was the hired caretaker responsible. It was winter, and in winter one doesn't expect a man—four men in this case—to go out in the cold and check on the welfare of caged, wild animals. Humane society agents had investigated reports, had gone out into the cold and plowed through the snow, saved the living and filed the charges. It's a wonder the three owners, professional men from fine families who regarded the game park as a side investment, didn't sue the humane society for defamation of character.

The little, commercial zoo isn't the only area where the humane movement knows almost complete frustration in its crusade to save wild as well as domestic animals from needless cruelties. It's next to impossible to bring the carnivals and small circuses to justice, for ownership must be established first, and by the time the maze of red tape has been cleared away, the enterprises have moved away to the next stop on their busy schedules. In addition, both operate in a manner that carries a built-in insurance against prosecution. This is known as local sponsorship. Volunteer fire departments, schools, worthy charities, churches—almost any group or institution except a humane society—are happy to sponsor and endorse the shows in return for a percentage of the profits or a flat payment. Or the reverse may be true, as in the case of the opening of a new shopping center where the show, in return for a flat payment, becomes a "free admission" come-on.

Granted a choice, the animals involved would probably prefer the small circus. Since it's bigger than the animal carnival, it employs more people, and there's always the chance that one of the hired hands has some basic knowledge of animal illness and care. Otherwise, there's not much choice between them. Both exist on small profits and overhead must be watched. It's more important to mend the tents and keep the old trucks running than it is to feed the animals. If the two-headed goat or the five-legged cow dies, it can be stuffed and exhibited in a glass case.

Rodeo promoters may have learned from the circus and the carnival that the public is willing to believe what it sees and ask no questions. The road-show customer accepts the bravery of the lion tamer, although the lion has neither teeth nor claws anymore. He applauds the dog in the high-wire act and doesn't suspect that the dog prefers walking above ground to being beaten on the ground. And if he notices the scars on the elephant's hide, he thinks they were made by jungle thorns and not bull-hooks.

It's always night when the show loads the trucks for the move to the next town. The public isn't there to see the big animals prodded, poled and beaten onto the trucks, or to watch the small ones being whipped into their crude shipping boxes.

Tens of thousands of animals live out their lives this way. Always on the move, always confined, never fed properly, abused into learning tricks, their health nobody's concern. They can't defend themselves and when they try to—as when the big cats, if they still retain teeth and claws, turn on their tormentor—they are shot.

Wild animals belong in the wild. If they must be confined, it should be in a respectable, legitimate zoo. Domestic animals belong at home, where it's tough enough for most. The roadside zoo, the small circus, the animal carnival—none of them belongs on the American scene. But there's no law that says so.

So the plight of the animals continues, everywhere and in all seasons.

The Ones Who Care 15

IN THE UNITED STATES, THE BEST FRIENDS OF THE ANI-mals are the humane societies. The patron saint of all the societies, national and local, is the late Henry Bergh, who originated the American humane movement by founding the American Society for Prevention of Cruelty to Animals (ASPCA). This first society was chartered in New York State.

A true animal lover, Bergh had been shocked by the maltreatment of domestic animals (particularly the horse) in Russia, where he served as a secretary for our legation. At the time, Russia had no anti-cruelty-to-animals laws, nor did the United States. He could do nothing about Russia, of course, but he was determined to do something here.

Bergh was full of concrete plans when he returned to the United States, for he came back via England, the one country in the world of that time with existing anti-cruelty laws. The humane movement there started in the eighteenth century, when Jeremy Bentham, the philosopher and jurist, pressed for legislation to protect animals from cruel treatment by humans. It should be of interest to biology teachers that Bentham maintained that if children were taught kindness to animals, they would be less likely to turn to future violence and crimes.

Bentham's crusade took a long time getting anywhere, but its first real victory finally came in 1822. The Ill-Treatment of Cattle Bill became law in that year. It called for fine or imprisonment of anyone judged guilty of cruelty to cattle and beasts of burden. Within two years, the world's first humane society was founded: The English Society for the Prevention of Cruelty to Animals. By royal command in 1840, this became the Royal Society. By then, the group had the sport of bull-baiting on the run and was not limiting its protection to cattle and beasts of burden. It was largely responsible for the Cruelty to Animals Act of 1849, which has since become the working model for humane laws all over the world: "If any person shall from and after the passing of this Act cruelly beat, ill-treat, overdrive, abuse or torture, or cause or procure to be cruelly beaten, ill-treated, over-driven, abused or tortured any animal, every offender shall for every such offense forfeit, and pay a penalty not exceeding five pounds." The law covered all domestic animals, and if it had any loopholes, they were plugged by a new law in 1854.

This is the one Henry Bergh brought home as a guide. He founded and became the first president of the ASPCA, thus launching the official humane movement in this country. The year was 1866, and New York State wasted no time in passing an anti-cruelty-to-animals law. In the next three years, humane societies and state anticruelty laws became facts in Massachusetts, New Jersey, California, Pennsylvania, Illinois and Minnesota. Now, a century later, all of the states have them.

To repeat: New York was the first of all our states

to pass anticruelty laws. Today—a hundred years later —the state still has the anticruelty laws, and a stranger visiting there will have no trouble finding racetracks, kosher slaughterhouses, animal dealers' farms, livestock auctions, roadside zoos, pesticide programs, bountied animals, vets who crop and dock dogs, rodeos, animal carnivals, and cruelty in research laboratories and public-school biology classes. If the stranger asks directions of the right people, he can also find cockfights and dog-fights.

Oddly, New York's anticruelty laws have served humans better than animals. Back in 1874, an ASPCA agent used the laws to rescue a child from her abusive foster mother. There were no laws anywhere to protect children from cruelty, and ASPCA acted on the theory that humans are animals. The theory worked, the foster mother was prosecuted and imprisoned, and soon New York became the first state to enact laws for the protection of children. All this led to the formation of the New York Society for the Prevention of Cruelty to Children, the first of its kind in the world. The year was 1876, and everything that's happened since then to better a child's life in this country and many other countries can be traced back to that year and the anticruelty laws for animals.

To repeat: child emancipation started in New York State where, not quite a century later, children in biology classes are taught many new methods of cruelty to animals. None of them realizes that if it weren't for the animals . . .

While all the above was going on, England was pushing ahead with more elaborate controls for the defense of animals. The whole country was embroiled in a debate over vivisection, or the rights of science versus the rights of animals. Parliament appointed several commissions to study the pros and cons, and one of them sat for six years before reporting on the answers of sixty experts who replied to over twenty thousand questions. In due time (1876), the law of 1854 was revamped and extended to regulate the practice of vivisection and outlaw needless cruelties in the laboratories. But the new anticruelty law had its loophole, for it covered only domesticated animals. The remedy came in 1900, and since then all animals in Britain, the domesticated ones and the wild ones in captivity, have enjoyed protection from needless abuse.

In terms of anticruelty laws, England remains years and miles ahead of the United States. Here we have absolutely no control over what goes on in the laboratories, and science remains unconcerned. But if humaneness is ever introduced into the labs, the humane societies will deserve a major share of the credit. They have not been alone in the struggle, but they've been the most consistent.

The United States war between the societies and the laboratories is over a century old now, and things are pretty much the same as they always have been: pick a lab at random, investigate it (if you can), and the odds are a hundred to one that you'll find the housing and treatment of the animals deplorable.

The minimum objective of the societies is the assurance that the laboratories will adopt and maintain standards of care for animals both before and after experiments. If just the labs operating with federal grants would do this, it would be a great victory, appreciated by thousands of humanitarians and millions of now suffering animals.

The maximum objective of the societies is that the laboratories apply common sense in their experiments with animals. There is no objection to qualified, humane experiments and there never has been. But once the results of an experiment have been discovered, and then adequately established, why keep on repeating it? And why use animals at all in the many cases when the results won't prove a thing for humans, as, for example, the present Food and Drug Administration tests on dogs to prove, or disprove, the cancerous effects of birth control pills?

Unfortunately for the animals, the world of science has been able to distort the aims of the humane societies, and the result is that about half of the general public believes that the societies are dead set against vivisection. Such is not the case. Where there is reason to hope that vivisection will somehow benefit man, most humane societies recognize it as valid. A campaign to abolish animal experimentation altogether is waged by the many antivivisection organizations both in this country and abroad. While these organizations are certainly a part of the humane movement, vivisection is their major concern and they regard all forms as criminal and immoral.

Thus the role of the humane society in the battle

with the laboratories is never quite clear, and nowhere is it more confused than in New York State, home of the first humane society and the first state anticruelty laws. A new law, the Metcalf-Hatch Bill, has now been added to the confusion. This law permits laboratories to requisition animals from ASPCA, which handles the pound activities for the City of New York. The Society knows all about what goes on in the laboratories, of course. Further, the Society's charter specifies that it exists for the *prevention* of cruelties to animals. Thus ASPCA is in a fix, and so is the whole national humane movement, for city pounds can be cheap sources of supply for the laboratories. So humane societies are worried, and so are the animal dealers.

The trouble with the legislators who passed the Metcalf-Hatch Bill (humanitarians refer to it as the "Hatchet-the-Calf Bill") may have been their misunderstanding of the functions of humane societies. All of them, whether purely local or affiliated with a national body, are dedicated to the prevention of cruelty to animals. And all of them may be considered private organizations, for they are supported by endowments and gifts. The taxpayer's taxes don't support the humane societies. Indeed, the societies save money for the taxpayers in many a community. For example, the societies are the reason that the old-fashioned animal pound (usually called the "dog pound") has been disappearing from the scene. The operation of the public pound was usually a local disgrace, and most of the public pounds that still exist haven't improved on that reputation. These days, for humanitarian, political and economic reasons, the progressive civic authorities have turned over the pound activities to the local humane society. For this public service, the society does receive a small fee. But the biggest small fee in the nation saves a community the much larger expense of running a pound, and it doesn't make a dent in the society's overhead: salaries for experienced staff members and veterinarians, equipment, ambulances, educational material for schools, property and buildings, and a hundred other costs.

But whether they operate a public pound or not, all humane societies have a code that governs the disposition of animals who enter their shelters: (1) return the animal to its rightful owner; (2) failing that, find a new and suitable home for the animal; and (3) failing that, give the animal (often diseased or injured) a merciful end.

It's the third point, perhaps, that confused the New York legislators and the nonthinking man in the street. If the animal is going to die anyway, why not hand him over to the laboratory or the biology teacher? Because the key word is "merciful," and no amount of distortion can change it to "torturous" or "cruel."

It's as simple as that. If you need a rabbit to train a Greyhound, or a dog to fight a dog, or a cat for a biology class, don't go to a humane society. But if you seek a pet and will give him a loving home, then you are most welcome there.

Hope for the Future? 16

THE OPPRESSED ARE HELPLESS. ANIMALS CANNOT TALK or vote or defend themselves in any way. But humans are not. They can do something about easing the plight of the animals in this country, if they care enough.

Americans would do well to imitate the English example. It's not that the English are by nature less cruel than we. It's just more expensive for an Englishman to be cruel to animals. The British courts respect the Royal Society for the Prevention of Cruelty to Animals, and heavy fines are imposed upon guilty parties. In addition, the non-humanitarian may find himself legally prohibited from owning or possessing any animals. Such sentences may run for five or ten years, or even for one's lifetime.

Thus in all the British Isles one will not find a single United States-style dealer's farm, livestock auction, animal carnival, roadside zoo, or biology class. While dog and cock fights are not unknown, they are infrequent, and those who stage them soon retire to prison cells. The medical research laboratories continue to use animals, of course, but while the animals are not treated like pampered pets, it would seem that way to dogs who have miraculously survived just one experiment in this country. Cattle and sheep and swine go to their deaths in England's slaughterhouses, but none must endure preliminary agonies.

There are examples of reform in this country, too, although they are rare and imperfect. In enlightened Connecticut, for instance, a man doesn't just plunk down a fee and obtain a hunting license. He must first prove that he knows how to handle a gun or attendance at state classes on gun handling is compulsory. In this one state the hunter, his wife, his family, and his neighbors have some protection against those all too numerous hunting season "accidents."

Though this may not help the wildlife very much, it can be regarded as progress toward the next logical step, the teaching of marksmanship. When the man who knows how to shoot a gun can use it with a fair degree of accuracy, then more wildlife will at least be spared the agonies of slow death. Thus far, none of our states has launched such a program, for it involves cost, and non-hunting taxpayers feel that enough is already being done for the hunters. But taxpayers will cheer any state enterprise that shows a profit, and one of these days perhaps a state will charge a fee for compulsory attendance at marksmanship school before issuing a hunting license. The man who can afford to hunt can easily afford a fee.

This reform achieved, it's a short distance to compulsory courses in target identification. All of our states require drivers to know the meaning of red, green, and yellow lights, and of road signs that identify curves, crossroads, and areas of falling stones. Yet not a single state requires a hunter to identify precisely what he's trying to kill. The average hunter should be able to distinguish a goose from a swan, a pheasant from a chicken, a deer from a cow, and any form of wildlife from a man. But he can't.

A measure of relief for wildlife, though indirectly gained, appears to be forthcoming. Pending legislation to restrict the sale and use of firearms (legislation born of man's inhumanities to man) can't help hurting the hunters—the eight million illegal ones, at any rate. And there is a piece of good news that nobody can explain: the total number of hunting licenses issued in several states has dropped in the last two years.

Progress is also being made on the pesticide problem. Old pesticides may remain, but new and deadlier ones won't be flooding the market. It takes a couple of years and up to three million dollars to develop a new one, and then the manufacturer must win the approval of the Department of Agriculture, which tests the product in its own fashion. These federal tests use up several generations of dogs, but when the pesticide is not approved, then they haven't suffered in vain, for millions of other animals will live.

At the state level, some progress has been made in bringing the abusive pesticides under control. New Hampshire was the first to outlaw the use of DDT on all state lands. Michigan has banned its use in state parks and avoids, as much as possible, the use of any persistent pesticide on state lands and game areas. Minnesota now restricts the use of pesticides on state lands. California, with its state lands under control, is bringing private interests into line by requiring permits for those who want to use the dangerous pesticides; the permits aren't easy to obtain and violaters are investigated and prosecuted; the law has teeth.

There's been a great deal of debate in some Eastern states: New York, Connecticut, Massachusetts and Maine. But the results have been negative, for those old American bedfellows, politics and private interests, continue to have their way.

Overall, the states have been lagging. Only about thirty have appointed pesticide control boards, and all but five of these boards are merely advisory. Thus twenty states are doing nothing at all, and twenty-five more are waiting for advice from control boards that have set new records for inactivity. One good reason for the lack of action, to say nothing about lack of advice, is that the strangest people serve on the advisory boards: such pesticide lovers as farmers, lawyers representing big business, big businessmen, and bankers who underwrite farmers and industry. Biologists, conservationists and ecologists—all of them long on sound advice—seem to be in short supply in some states. Still, a few states have seen the light; others are bound to follow.

The horrors of the slaughterhouse would end tomorrow if everyone stopped eating meat and substituted fish. It won't happen, of course, but at least the state of Iowa, now in the Humane Slaughter Law column, is backing the federal law with more than words, and that's one more state than there was in 1966. The states may not be able to do anything about ritual slaughter, but slaughterhouses could have a change of mind if retailers refused to sell their products.

In the world of entertainment—films, television, and rodeo—the codes are still being ignored. But the proper treatment of animals in American-made films and in rodeos could be assured through state supervision. All the states have anticruelty laws, though only one state—Ohio—enforces them. But one state is a little progress in the right direction. A few years ago, no state was interested.

Even the shamefully mistreated laboratory animal is beginning to receive some attention. Congress did pass the Laboratory Animal Welfare Act (1966), and then weakened it before the Act could become law, so that conditions for the animals haven't improved. The law is aimed at the suppliers of laboratory animals, not at the abuses performed in the laboratories at federal expense. But protest can bring results, as witness the Rat Control Bill. Congress rejected that bill, until it heard from the folks back home; then it reversed itself. Enough loud voices could bring about improvement of the Laboratory Act as well.

In the long run, the needless, senseless suffering of our animals won't diminish to any significant degree unless and until a far greater proportion of our adults take an active interest. The humane groups are doing their part, but they can't be everywhere. Activity requires very little time and no money. For example, more often than not, there are diseased animals at the average roadside zoos, animal carnivals, dealer farms, and livestock auctions. Over one hundred animal diseases can be transmitted to man, and every local board of health knows this. Unfortunately, most of these boards are content with routine duties, which amount to checking rather than preventing the spread of disease. In most states, they can be pried from their chairs by written complaints. By law, they must investigate every complaint filed by a citizen. When it's a matter of human health, the boards have the authority to put the tawdry animal businesses out of business and to cause arrests. Where the state is lax, and the local authorities don't seem to care, the boards can save the day. But first the complainers must make themselves heard.

The greatest single stumbling block to progress is big business. The federal agencies often know what to do and how to do it, and they have both the capabilities and the funds. But they operate under laws that contain an astonishing number of loopholes, and always they are up against an army of influential profiteers: the ranchers, the packers, the makers of chemicals, and all the others who want things to continue in the good old American way, because it's a golden way for them. They resent change and restrictions. They act as though we still have plenty of everything, and we don't.

Big business made this country strong and great, and only fools don't want it. But it has neither royal nor divine right to continue its reckless ways: dumping deadly chemicals into our waters, poisoning the fertile land and all that grows and feeds on it, raping our forests and filling our wetlands—and recklessly slaughtering our animals.

Big business must listen or be forced to listen, and then its reasonable men will change their traditional ways. They will listen, and so will Washington, when the citizens raise their voices in protest.

There are indications that we have entered a period of creeping awareness of our past and current follies, and ultimately this awareness must benefit our animal life. Now many people are trying to do something about air and water pollution, and one day these abuses will come to an end. Many others are concerned about the disappearing forests and wetlands. Yesterday, conservation and ecology were just words, and today they have meaning for millions.

The nation's press is full of editorials pleading for corrections and demanding federal laws to preserve the natural resources that still remain. The books are pouring off the presses and warning all who care to read that there won't be a happy tomorrow unless we call a halt to the destruction of today. And confused as many of our federal agencies may be (some don't know where their jurisdiction begins or ends, and several overlap), all are determined to save what we have and then go on from there.

And this awareness is beginning to be extended to our animal life. The press and the magazines are devoting more space to exposing the cruelties to animals. Every year, a few more politicians stand up to be counted on the side of the animal lovers, knowing full well that they risk losing the votes of big business and special interest groups.

This new awareness of the necessity of conserving our resources may be dictated by self-interest, but self-interest means self-preservation, and this will be best achieved through kindness. And fortunately kindness, unlike the passenger pigeon, is not extinct. Man is learning that by hurting others—humans or animals—he is only hurting himself.

Index